ELEMENTS OF
ENGLISH
ARCHITECTURE

ELEMENTS OF
ENGLISH
ARCHITECTURE

HUGH BRAUN

DAVID & CHARLES : NEWTON ABBOT

0 7153 5775 1

Set in eleven on thirteen point Imprint
and printed in Great Britain
by Latimer Trend & Company Ltd Plymouth
for David & Charles (Holdings) Limited
South Devon House Newton Abbot Devon

CONTENTS

LIST OF ILLUSTRATIONS

PLATES

IN TEXT

PREFACE

NOTHING PLAYS a more important part in the visible history of a country than its architecture. Not always the large buildings towering above city streets, nor even the country mansions that can be glimpsed here and there between the trees of their parks, for these were often the creations of a sophisticated, perhaps even international, style of architecture. It is the homes of ordinary people, set amongst the fields of farmlands or scattered along village streets, which illustrate the real architecture of a country. Churches, large or small, form a special study, as do also the archaic fortresses of the Middle Ages. But the story of the English home starts at the beginning, goes on unchecked through centuries of history, and remains beside us as we journey through the country.

These buildings bear no trace of the work of the professional architect. Not until the Middle Ages had faded into history could one even find builders for them. The European Renaissance had been under way for some two centuries before the modern house, builder-constructed, began to take its place in England. Prior to this, the ordinary English home was essentially a do-it-yourself job of poles and thatch, hardly architecture, but at least a roof over the heads of the peasant and his family.

At this time, of course, the home of the lord of the manor was builder-constructed and a fine house for its day. Today we call such houses 'cottages'. But the real cottages of the Middle Ages have perished long ago under the fern and bracken or been ploughed back again into the soil whence they sprang.

While few people build their own houses these days, the do-it-yourself interest is strongly displayed by people who want to alter or enlarge their homes. These amateurs may no more need architects than their predecessors who built the original house. And as they work, the novice builders find themselves learning a great deal about the building methods of other days.

Rural buildings reflect the spirit of the countryside in which they stand. Indeed they are often built of the same materials as those from which nature constructed their surroundings. England displays many varieties of scenery. The most striking features of the South are the high downlands lying from west to east across such counties as Wiltshire and Buckinghamshire, and across Sussex. Through their chalky soils run veins of flint from which so many of their buildings are constructed. As the chalk spreads across East Anglia it provides flint for building there also. North and west of the chalk reaches the great limestone highland which passes from Somerset into Northamptonshire through the Cotswold country with its famous stone architecture. The primeval woodland which once covered the fertile Midlands and the East Anglian plain has been felled and turned into timber-framed houses as famous in their way as the houses of the Cotswolds. The western end of the limestone belt dissolves into a tumbled region linking it to the rocky moors of the West Country which find a distant echo in the wild moorland hills of the North.

The pattern of 'coloured counties' which makes up the English countryside is everywhere before us. They are the fields of meadow, pasture and corn, roots and plough and fallow which form the patchwork of the farmers' lands. Here and there a pastoral park sprinkled with trees surrounds the home of a country squire at the end of its tall avenue. And above the cultivation rise the bare crests of wold and downland, often crowned by clumps of trees, planted perhaps a century or two ago by the squire to celebrate the birth of an heir or the news of a victory.

England is a land of trees—of oak and ash and thorn, beech and elm and chestnut. Groups of them nearly always give shelter to farmhouse and hamlet. Sometimes they climb the hillsides to crown their summits with mystery. And everywhere are the deep coverts where deer once browsed unseen.

Threading the countryside are the streams, the wild torrents of the West and the placid waters that sweep towards the North Sea. Beside them stand countless mills, their wheels for the most part long vanished, but their houses forming today some of the most enchanting of our rural homes.

Everywhere are the farmhouses, their origins for the most part lying deep in the days of the Tudors. Many of them have been divided up into cottages for labourers and many again are in process of being restored to their former integrity. In various stages of historical development they line the village streets and cluster round their greens. Some have now been absorbed into towns where, considered unsuitable as urban residences, they try to survive demolition. For a time their roofs of thatch, warm tile, and grey stone hold their own amongst concrete replacements, but day by day the survivors fall victims to progress—and English architecture becomes the poorer for their loss.

Not only the national architecture but its regional styles play a prominent part in the variety of the English scene, each contributing vitality to the tapestry. With the countryside diversified by a constantly changing subsoil, each region produces, as well as a change of scenery, a different type of architecture. Close to the stone building of the Cotswolds with its heavy stone roofs and mullioned windows are the black-and-white 'magpie' houses covering the West Midland plain and the Marcher lands which border Wales. The flint walling of the Downs is intermingled with framed houses of timber grown on the soil of the valleys.

In the remote wildernesses of West and North one finds the grim moorstone homes half carved out of the rocky hillsides, their greyness often relieved by a dressing of white. And in the hinterland of the North Sea coast, wool from East Anglian sheep was exchanged for warm red brick imported from the Low Countries.

It will probably be these regional characteristics which will create the greatest interest in the mind of the reader. Those of his home country will predominate in his thoughts, or those of the regions he visits when on carefree holiday. His knowledge of the former, the developments of its structural devices in particular, he will best be able to appreciate, while his examination of the others will possibly be limited to their external appearance.

Many English people live in old houses and have the opportunity of acquiring a deep knowledge of their architecture for no other reason than that it is always producing items requiring maintenance. These fortunate people will be more particularly interested in Chapter 1 of this book. For those who have to admire from a distance Chapter 3 tries to present the history of elevational architecture in England. People who inhabit or visit English houses may well be interested in the story of the changes in the house plan as outlined in Chapter 2. The present writer hopes that those about to build anew may be interested in the technical details of architectural design, some of which are set forth in Chapter 5. In particular, he hopes that every building raised in the days to come will be carefully considered, not only as a home for the owner, but as something which will add to the serenity of town, village, or countryside, that the continuing beauty of England may be assured.

As the reader follows the history of the English house from the fifteenth to the eighteenth century he may gradually begin to appreciate the significance of the many and varied units, each having its own particular fascination, which go to make up the architectural composition, whether it be a 'row of cottages' or the frontage of one of those village streets the like of which for charm of appearance and historical interest may be seen nowhere else in the world.

Everyone knows those pictorial views of Old England as they appear on postcards and calendars. Everyone takes them for granted, accepting them as the townsman accepts his morning milk in bottles without a thought for the cow. But piece by piece these enchanting vistas are being whittled away, many in the course of that operation which we know as 'development' . . . which in fact more often than not represents sheer destruction.

Perhaps if we could understand better just what these 'cottages' mean, consider their origins and purpose and their long struggle to survive through the passing centuries, they may become more real to us. Living history—their bricks and tiles, whitewash and thatch—can tell a story to those who want to hear it.

And what of the intruders upon their history, new neighbours so often slapped down beside them without any consideration—according them no courtesy and seeming to mock, rather than respect, their antiquity? A respect for the works of his forebears is an attitude which the architect of today might consider worth cultivating.

The example set us by the architectural profession is nowadays open to criticism. And what has now become a really alarming feature of the expansion of English bureaucracy is the astonishing anomaly that all building designs have to be approved by local government bodies whose members have themselves no knowledge of architecture whatsoever, neither as regards systems of construction nor the way in which buildings are aesthetically presented to the public view. The writer hopes that the following pages may in some measure help responsible councillors to form a better idea of the nature of English architecture, particularly in connection with those national characteristics which play such a vital part in presenting to the outside world the image of England.

H.B.

CHAPTER ONE

ENGLISH HOUSE CONSTRUCTION

THE TWO factors upon which the architectural style of a region is based are, firstly, the climatic conditions against which the house-builder has to contend, and secondly, the materials at hand with which he can work.

The climate of England is one of the most trying in the world. The rain is cold and lacks a warm sun to follow and dry out the ground and the structures raised upon it. Strong winds combine to drive the rains into the interstices of walls and roofing. Constant damp breeds fungoid growths which bring about decay in timber and thatch and carry chemical substances which cause decay in stone and brick. Thus even buildings of permanent construction cannot survive to the same age as those of Mediterranean antiquity, while timber and thatch are so ephemeral that a whole fine architectural style, that of the Anglo-Saxon carpenters, perished long ago without trace.

The most severe component of the English climate is its winter snowfall. The damp snow clings to buildings and saturates them; it blows into crevices and increases the humidity of the interior of the house. Thus a basic factor in English building was the employment of every device possible to keep snow from adhering.

Another dangerous aspect of the damp snow in England is its great weight. It is curious how many drawings and models of prehistoric timber huts one finds in museums—seemingly based upon

Kaffir kraals—which would have collapsed upon the heads of their occupants with the first snowfall of winter!

Even with permanent buildings, snow has to be taken into consideration. The flat roofs covered with boards and mud which are universal in the Mediterranean region would not survive under English snowfall. A steep roof which offers no hold to snow and sends it sliding earthward is the appropriate roof for an English building. This element in English architecture is so fundamental that we shall find that it was originally the roof which made the house, walls being merely an added luxury.

The whole purpose of the early house being to keep out the winter weather, any openings made through the house's defences were kept as small as possible. The first doorways were so low as to necessitate a crawling entry as into an igloo. Interior lighting being of small value to people who could not read, windows were not required, even those to such important buildings as churches being mere slits through which a minimum of light could filter. The weak spot in the house being its entrance doorway, wherever possible extra defences were added to it in the form of a porch. The purpose of this was to deflect from the doorway any winds blowing from its flanks or above, leaving only those directly aimed to do their worst. The porch is an essentially English feature, virtually unknown in warmer climes; it comes into its own during the great days of the Gothic, to be abandoned for a time with the introduction of foreign architecture after the end of the sixteenth century.

A vital part of the equipment of the English house has always been its fire-hearth. This had to be inside the building so that in addition to being used for cooking in bad weather it could also keep the occupants warm. For many centuries the smoke from the fire was allowed to gather in the rafters and drift down as it cooled, to the discomfort of those below—who may have had to take turns at going to the doorway for a breath of air. Eventually a breach in the defences had to be contrived high in the roof to allow the smoke to escape without letting the rain in.

The eventual solution to the smoke problem was found to be the introduction of the wall-fireplace, having above it a 'tunnel' to draw away the smoke. The ends of these tunnels projecting above the roof became the chimneys which are such a notable feature of English domestic architecture, differentiating this entirely from the domestic architecture found in the Mediterranean region where fires are for cooking only.

While in important English houses chimneys existed as early as the eleventh century, it was not until the end of the sixteenth century that their use became universal, a forest of them suddenly appearing throughout the towns and countryside of England. The separate flues did not however remain for long, being gathered together under the influence of the chimney-less Renaissance into the solid chimney stack familiar to us today.

We have remarked that in England the roof is the house. It is not the covering-over of wall-tops, but the actual shelter itself.

When the writer was a boy and used to walk in the 'green lanes' of England, he would often watch the gypsies building their simple 'tans'. They would plant two rows of willow or hazel rods into holes punched with an iron bar, bending them inwards towards each other so that they could be tied together where they met to form the ribs of a tunnel (Fig 1). Over this framework they threw a covering of sacking or old blankets; sometimes this again was covered with bracken or furze, to make a cosy home for the gypsy family. One end of the tan was covered over, and before the other was the fire of twigs over which they had to step when entering or leaving.

It seems likely that, in a country blessed with ample supplies of standing timber rising above dense undergrowth, many early houses may have been constructed in this fashion. They would of course have lasted only for a few months before having to be renewed, which may explain the medieval chronicler's cynical comment on the sufferings of peasantry whose homes had been destroyed during some military campaign. With a few poles, he said, they would soon have homes again. Of all this mass of vanished timber building nothing remains save filled-in foundation holes awaiting the trowel and teaspoon of the archaeological excavator.

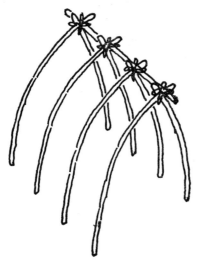

Fig 1
Gypsy 'tan'
Two parallel rows of hazel wands set into the ground, bent towards each other and secured to ridge-pole, covered with sacking and thatched bracken, etc

One of the haunting mysteries of English history is the real nature of the Roman occupation of Britain. We know that during their four centuries of sojourn they raised fine cities in the style, if not the scale, of Imperial Rome. Practically every vestige of all this architectural achievement has vanished—probably long ago burnt for lime. The rural 'villas'—those verandahed bungalows seemingly so curiously unsuited to the English climate—were slightly constructed and probably soon fell into ruin after their owners had sailed away to Rome leaving behind them their wonderful carpets of mosaic.

Of the homes of the native inhabitants during these four centuries we know little, but experience suggests that they continued to represent purely local effort and tradition, in exactly the same way as we have seen the native village reaching away from the Imperial cantonment in the African bush. That the long Roman occupation appears to have had no effect upon the architectural development of England seems understandable when we realise that architecture needs builders and that only the Romans themselves could have afforded to employ these, importing them from Rome and taking them back with them.

From the tan-type of house developed an important style of architecture which has lasted longer with us. Replacing the willow-wands with stouter poles prevented these being bent before they were tied together at the apex of the structure, so that the 'tunnel' became a triangular tent having little headroom down the sides. So the next development was to select curved poles in order to restore the tunnel-like section of the tan. In this way developed the important style of architecture based upon the timber 'cruck' (Fig 2), that wishbone of curved beams which when set side by side manage to combine the functions of wall and roof in one sweep.

Fig 2
Crucks Heavy curved timbers pinned together in pairs to form framework of hall of Anglo-Saxon days

The cruck system of building seems to have been developed by the Anglo-Saxons, and it is tempting to suggest that it may have been the practice of making homes out of derelict boats turned upside down on the beach which led to the invention of the rib-like crucks. The system was developed during the Dark Ages until it achieved the scale of a royal hall such as has been excavated at Cheddar in Somerset. The Bayeux tapestry shows that in the days of King Edward the Confessor Westminster Hall was of cruck construction.

The system survived in England into the seventeenth century, by which time the bowed timbers had been replaced by angled ones (Fig 3), indicating a clear distinction between the roof of the structure and the walling below it.

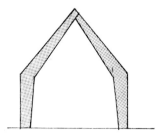

Fig 3
Later type of cruck
Formed from trunk of tree and lowermost
branch, taking shape of wall and roof; continues
in use until end of seventeenth century

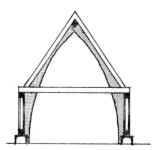

Fig 4
Cruck construction
The cruck provided with a tie-beam the ends of
which support timber screen-walls. The apex
of the truss carries ridge-pieces which support
rafters springing from heads of timber screens

Such an architectural style as this could only have been developed in a country possessing plenty of forest timber. Nevertheless the style was a primitive one and could not have survived indefinitely against pressure from the more sophisticated building fashions which had in antiquity established as a principle the building of a wall and the covering of it with a roof. For although the Anglo-Saxons had made notable progress in roof construction, they now had to face the problem of how to raise a wall.

Taking as a basis the massive curved cruck which combined the functions of roof and wall, the problem resolved itself into how to separate the two component parts. The roof was left alone, the lower part of the cruck being replaced by a separate vertical post. This was a revolutionary step. Hitherto unknown problems in stability had to be faced, in practice by employing extremely massive timbers. The Anglo-Saxons applied themselves to the task of raising a wall and thus brought their splendid timber architecture into line with that of the great achievements of antiquity.

Now that rafters and posts had become separated, there remained no longer any need to maintain the spacing of the rafters, kept narrow to carry their covering, when siting the posts. Thus the posts became fewer and more widely spaced, bringing upon each post a heavier load than it had carried hitherto. Since posts were beginning to sink into the ground under these loads a system was adopted of stepping them on continuous balks of timber like the keels of boats but of great size and strength to prevent settlement of the heavy building above (Fig 5).

Upon this posted framework the roof was raised, its rafters being carried down almost to ground level, in the same fashion as has since been followed by the timber barns which remain in their hundreds to this day, these in all probability representing fairly accurate copies of the pillared halls of twelfth-century England but with their timbers greatly reduced in scale. Imagine their timbering doubled in size and one may begin to understand something of the splendid timber architecture which could produce even tall churches—the wonder of Western Europe.

The timber foundations of these barns—their 'keels'—are set at right angles to the outer walls. In stoneless Essex we may still find timber bell-towers with their great posts, usually six in number, mounted upon keels some two feet square, running *down* the building, side by side, from west to east. Thus these tall structures, which are in fact planned as short but lofty churches, may actually be survivors of the original churches of Anglo-Saxon England. This system of architectural timber framing, developed for use in buildings of the first class, eventually came down to within the scope of the ordinary house-builder.

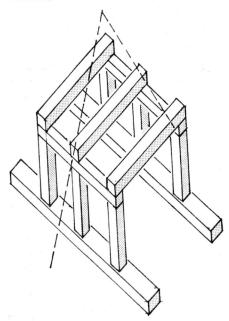

Fig 5
Posted construction
Opposing rows of posts set upon timber sills and joined together by lintels, the rows tied together by cross-beams; probably dating from Anglo-Saxon days

Posted construction is of course still removed from the traditional system of roofs carried upon walls. Indeed the actual walling of these buildings was simply formed of lightly-constructed screens or brattices formed of the rough boards left from the squaring of the great timbers. These boards were fixed in position by shaving down their ends and setting them at head and foot into grooves cut to receive them in horizontal timbers (as may still be seen at Greensted church in Essex). The spaces between the boards could be stuffed with clay; another method was to face them alternately so that each board covered a gap

Page 25 (*right*) The prominent feature of this farmhouse at Aldenham in Hertfordshire is the gable of its cross-chamber, the wing set athwart the main building and containing the great parlour with the great chamber above. A timber-built descendant of the thirteenth-century manor house, the close timbering indicates an early sixteenth-century date with the square-panelled work representing repairs of perhaps a century later. The original chimney stack can be seen; (*below*) a yeoman's house at Bignor in Sussex displaying a neatly contrived plan with a central hall and a pair of cross-chambers formed by jettying out the joists of their upper floors. The symmetry of the design suggests the influence of the Renaissance and the square-panelled framing suggests a late sixteenth-century date

Page 26 (*above*) A fine house at Houghton in Huntingdonshire with its upper storey jettied throughout. The Elizabethan chimney stack has lost the Classical caps which originally crowned the flues of kitchen, parlour, and chamber; (*below*) Sandford Orcas in Dorset lies on the fringe of the belt of limestone which produced the notable architecture of Somerset and the Cotswolds. A perfect little manor house of the opening years of the sixteenth century, its hall-door is covered by a tower-porch but the hall itself has shrunk to give place to an impressive cross-chamber having the hall bay transferred to it and designed to light the great parlour with its chamber above. The appearance of a lower cross-chamber indicates the influence of Renaissance symmetry

Page 27   (*above*) The great
Jacobean mansion of Barrington
Court in Somerset, built about 1515,
shows the medieval manor house
enlarged by the addition of a second
cross-chamber and the pair extended
to form long wings. The tower-
porch remains, set in the centre of
the composition in complete
acceptance of Renaissance symmetry.
Note the relics of medievalism in the
chimney stacks and the gable
finials; (*left*) the manor house of
Nether Lypiatt in Gloucestershire
illustrates Dutch domestic architecture of about the year 1700
introduced into England to lay the
foundations of the Georgian architecture of the eighteenth century.
Note the replacement of gables by a
completely hipped roof, the plain
Renaissance chimney stacks, and the
sash windows divided into small
panes

Page 28 (*above*) At Faringdon House in Berkshire the squire's home of about 1780 has become a completely international Renaissance villa complete with pedimented façade and balustraded parapet. The small pillared porch, however, remains as a very English feature of the house; (*below*) by 1778 Heveningham Hall in Suffolk has grown so huge that of its humble ancestor nothing is left but the name. This great Classical mansion spreads its colonnaded frontispiece, from wing to wing, across the squire's park to advertise the majesty of Regency England

left between two neighbours—a system followed today in the erection
of hovels.

All the building devices described above depend upon a supply of
forest timber such as could once have been found covering most of the
centre of England and its south and eastern coasts. To the north and
west, however, lay bare timberless regions.

Much of the material used in building was gathered when land was
being cleared for agricultural purposes. The trees of the forest became
barns for the storage of grain grown on their sites. The tremendous
architecture of the great stone monuments of the Megalithic Age
developed with the clearance of rocky land for farming. And in countryside such as the Cotswolds the rough pieces of field-stone that cluttered
the ground could be collected and put to use for building homes.

The technique employed in using stone for building was of course
entirely different from that followed in timber construction. Roof
timbers of a sort could be gathered in from poor-quality woodland but
could hardly be compared with the true building-timber coming out
of the stately oak-forests. But the builders could make use of piles of
field-stone for walling, and in this way approach nearer to the traditional
system of architectural building which set a roof upon walls.

In fact the rough walling of prehistoric days served a quite different
purpose. It would have been impossible to bury the feet of timber
crucks in a rocky soil, but the piles of field-stone arranged in the form
of walls provided adequate matrices in which the feet of rafters could
be buried (Fig 6). At first merely poles, with the development of
building techniques these became sturdier timbers and were often
selected curved, in the manner of crucks, in order to achieve greater
head-room. It is however incorrect to describe wall-mounted timbers as
crucks, for the true cruck rises from the ground and serves as wall-post
as well as rafter. As time went on, cruck houses came to be provided with
walls arranged around them and helping them to carry the roof. Such
walls could be built of field-stone or brick. Another system was to run a
tie-beam across the cruck from side to side and project the ends so that
these might carry the head-timbers of boarded screen-walls or brattices

(Fig 4). It is usually these houses which have survived to the present day, some of them built as recently as the seventeenth century (but possibly of second-hand crucks).

Fig 6
Stone hut
Where poles cannot be set in rocky ground a ring of
large stones is raised and feet of poles buried in it.
Remains of these houses are the 'hut circles' of Britain's
moorlands

Walls of field-stone cannot be made to join in salient angles without the risk that these will fall away and drop off. Thus the early homes built of such material were usually circular on plan with pole-supported roofs covering them. These were the 'beehive huts' of prehistory, the ruined 'hut circles' of which many yet remain scattered about the bare rocky plains of the West and North.

The humble hut circles remain as memorials of those rock-bound homes, while the great volume of timber architecture, great and humble, has long vanished.

A building material of international fame is common mud or—as it is called in England—cob. The Baghdad of Harun el Raschid was entirely built of it, made into bricks and dried in the sun. The writer has ridden over its site, today a bare plain: palaces, mosques, great walls and gates . . . all have returned to the desert whence they sprang.

In Britain only certain soils can be made into cob. A wonderful material, it is immensely tough and if protected from erosion by stormwater will survive for centuries. It was still being used in the 1920s. But its speedy collapse if neglected has resulted in the loss of so many buildings that its antiquity in England cannot be determined. As it cannot be employed without a good foundation of stone or brick to keep it from rising damp, excavation would undoubtedly expose the sites of many cob houses which have vanished from the surface of the land.

It is a long leap from the shelter of rubble stone to the stone building as we know it today. This is the product of a highly skilled craft, almost certainly imported from Europe, a craft which in its day was the most important trade to be found in the countryside.

It is important to be able to appreciate what constitutes building in stone. We sometimes read in descriptions of buildings that they are 'faced' with stone. Except in the special case of rough walling faced with slabs of stone this description is almost invariably wrong. What the writer was endeavouring to describe is a wall built in *masonry*, a very specialised form of wall-construction employed in the buildings of the Middle Ages and continuing until replaced by the craft of the bricklayer. Masonry walls are built in two skins of stone forming the wall-faces, the space between these being filled with the debris of the stone-cutting (see Fig 7). Mortar is employed to bed the facing stones

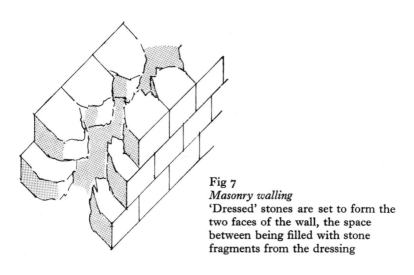

Fig 7
Masonry walling
'Dressed' stones are set to form the two faces of the wall, the space between being filled with stone fragments from the dressing

and help to consolidate the rough stone core. Masonry has provided the finest achievements of architecture.

The use of such skilled craftsmanship was quite outside the scope of the ordinary house-builder who would have to content himself with getting hold of pieces of dressed stone to form the quoins which held the angles of his walling firm. He might even be able to find dressed stones with which to form his door and window openings. But for the most part, such features and the services of the men to fix them would only have been procurable by the richest people. The ordinary man, still of necessity building his home by do-it-yourself methods, would have no chance at all of getting hold of a mason and paying him.

The medieval mason was the most highly paid tradesman in the country. There were no building firms in those days, and anyone needing a house had to assemble a team of masons—as well as carpenters, smiths, glaziers and so forth—from all over the country, and these men would walk or ride their ponies to the building site where they had to be housed and fed in temporary accommodation. The masons were provided with a 'lodge'—basically a lean-to structure attached to an existing building or the rising wall of a new one (from it derives the word 'lodging'). The master-mason was the head of the team of masons, and was responsible for setting out the building and organising the work.

The trade of masonry controlled all major English building until the sixteenth century when bricks began to appear in quantity. Large tile-like bricks had been made in millions by the Roman colonists and after their departure were wrenched out of the ruins of their buildings and used again and again for quoins and dressings generally. Fresh bricks first appeared during the thirteenth century as ballast in ships returning from carrying wool to the Low Countries. First used in important buildings in East Anglia, they were similar to those of today but only two-thirds of the thickness. No one in England knew how to lay them. The masons had always been careful to 'break joint' so that no two vertical joints arrived above one another to inaugurate a possible crack in the wall. The first 'red masons' who began to lay bricks in East Anglia seem to have been afraid that their little pieces of material would fall out of the wall so they laid them as headers, at right angles to the wall (Fig 8a) so that only a minimum of bonding was possible. Later they laid a course of stretchers between each course of headers (Fig 8b) in the 'English bond' which lasted until the end of the seventeenth century when it was replaced by the 'Flemish bond' (Fig 8c) in which we find each course laid with headers and stretchers alternating in the same course.

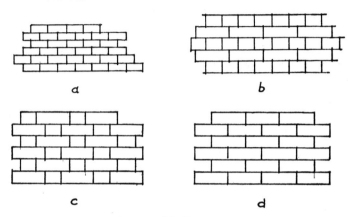

Fig 8
Brick 'bonding'
(a) 'Header bond' used for the thin bricks of Tudor days, (b) 'English bond' used in the seventeenth century, (c) 'Flemish bond' which took the place of English at the end of the century, (d) 'stretcher bond' used in the cavity walls of today

All these bricks, and those which were being manufactured in millions from 1600 or so onwards in Britain, were burnt in kilns using wood for fuel. But the great demand for bricks after World War I led to a new type of brick being manufactured by a process in which the brick instead of being burnt was squeezed in a giant press. This is the pressed brick of today which we see in every conceivable colour from white to black, mottled and flashed to every degree of 'artistry'.

Another form of walling material is concrete, made of an aggregate of sand and gravel bound together in a matrix of portland cement.

Cement is manufactured by mixing chalk and clay and baking in a kiln to form a material which when mixed with water will harden to a great degree of compressive strength. Concrete made of cement and aggregate may be reinforced by being formed around cores of steel rods to take up the tensional stresses which would shatter unreinforced concrete.

Concrete may be cast into portable blocks for erection into walling. If the aggregate used should be waste material such as cinders or coke breeze the result is a lightweight block of no great strength but easily portable and useful today for constructing internal partitions.

Walling built up of small pieces of stone or brick is much less likely to disintegrate if the material is set in a matrix of mortar. The mortar used in medieval times and until portland cement came into use in the mid-nineteenth century was formed with lime manufactured by burning limestone. The tall kilns in which this valuable material—used by the farmer for top-dressing his soil as well as by the builder in his walling—may be seen everywhere in a countryside where limestone exists in the soil. Inside these tall castle-like towers are the bottle-shaped kilns themselves and at their feet are the cavernous arches containing the firing doors which often still remain in position.

Mortar for bedding stone and bricks in a wall is composed of lime (its proportion varying with the integrity of the builder) slaked with water and mixed with sand. When looking at a fine building spreading its fronts of masonry before us, we are apt to forget the part played by mortar in keeping the high walls from falling into ruin.

The vital constituent of mortar being lime, which can only be burnt from limestone, we find the architectural aorta of England formed by the great limestone belt which runs from Somerset and Dorset north-eastwards through the Cotswolds, Northamptonshire and Lincolnshire to the East Riding of Yorkshire where the great abbey ruins stand, joined by the generous limestone to the Georgian glories of Bath.

Thus limestone not only forms the finest building stone but also provides the essential part of the mortar in which to set it. To the north and west of the limestone belt is good building sandstone, but this has to be fed with mortar from the limestone. The masons of the North and West who dwelt in the heart of the rock knew well how to fashion their intractable material into building blocks but were often too far away from sources of lime to be able to make mortar. So right up to the seventeenth century good stone houses in those regions had their material laid 'dry', having to wait for transport improvements to supply them with lime so that they could plaster over their walling inside and out.

Part of the architecture of the English countryside lies in its quarries, each of them representing a source of valuable material—each in its special region a centre of pilgrimage. Humblest are the sand quarries, to which the builder must perforce travel to gather one of the constituents of his mortar. Quarries for poor quality limestone for burning are next in importance. In areas such as the north-west Midlands where the building stone is sandstone we find the colourful quarries where this material is ready to be cut out and carried to the lodge where the stonemasons waited for it. Most important of all were the quarries yielding the fine freestone used for building great churches and castles across the main south-eastern mass of the country from Lincoln to Bath, first frontier of the invading legions of Rome.

In masonry walling, the two faces are constructed first (see Fig 7), so that the wall is raised completely faced. Brick walls are built in a single thickness, each course of bricks having its own faces, the bricks for which are sometimes specially selected for the task. Thus there is usually a difference between the 'common' brick and the 'face' brick, the latter being nowadays formed with every kind of texture and an infinite variety of colour.

Stone facing or ashlar—which it will be remembered is something quite different from masonry—has been applied to rough walling since the fifteenth century when it was used to cover up rubble work and by the eighteenth century was serving to face a wall built of common bricks. Ashlar varies from six to eight inches in thickness and is set on edge in much larger sizes than is seen in masonry work (see Fig 9).

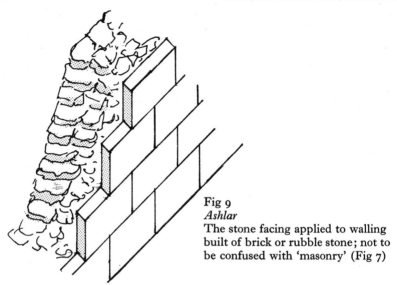

Fig 9
Ashlar
The stone facing applied to walling built of brick or rubble stone; not to be confused with 'masonry' (Fig 7)

Nowadays one sees a good deal of walling faced with an artificial stone formed of stone dust mixed into a paste with cement and water and cast in moulds. All kinds of imitation 'tooling' can be cast into the displayed face of the stone which can also copy rough rock or 'rustication'; strange colours can also be supplied.

Everyone has heard about the cement the Romans used—the present portland cement is of course a recent invention—and how it is believed to go on hardening for ever. 'Roman' cement was made by burning nodules of a natural cement found in certain clays. Like portland cement it will not erode, as lime will, when subjected to the scouring of rain, so the Romans made their mortar by mixing cement with the sand instead of using lime as in medieval days; thus their mortar was indeed much harder than ordinary masons' stuff.

A way of finishing the face of a wall the material of which might be regarded as too rough for dignity is to cover it with a rendering of cement and sand. While builders worked in lime mortar, however, a rendering of this material would soon deteriorate. It was not until the rediscovery of Roman cement late in the eighteenth century that the fronts of buildings began to be permanently rendered. To provide an illusion that the wall was ashlar-faced lines were often incised with a trowel to suggest the joints of stonework.

Before the invention of tarmacadam, the coaching roads of the turnpike era were surfaced with grit (well remembered by veterans of the cycling age!) and kept 'water-bound' either naturally or artificially. Wind, stormwater and the passage of vehicles constantly swept the road-grit into the roadside gutters whence it had to be cleared by the roadmen and stacked in piles on the verges. It was this material which was prized by the plasterers when covering the walls of houses with a Roman cement rendering. The grit was small in gauge and easily worked with the trowel to leave a smooth surface not unlike that of natural stone. What was most desirable was that it weathered like natural stone and soon produced a pleasant patina (such as could never appear on the portland cement renderings of today).

What today we call 'rendering' is the covering of a wall-face with a mixture of cement and sand applied with a flat smoothing tool made of iron or wood and called a float. Another form of rendering, however, sometimes known as scat, is applied by simply throwing lumps of pre-mixed cement and fine shingle on to the wall from a hand shovel, leaving the resultant lumps untouched by the float. The effect produced by this is of a rendering lightly applied to a rough rubble wall, an interesting texture unobtainable by ordinary rendering.

With the introduction of portland cement, what was called rough-cast came into use, but as the roadside grit had disappeared under the tar-sprays, a dreadful form of rendering appeared which was produced by throwing small-gauge shingle on to the wet rendering. This 'pebble-dash' became the sign-manual of early twentieth-century suburban architecture.

Nowadays we employ another popular form of rendering, known as Tyrolean, produced by blowing the compound on to the wall-face so that it settles into a kind of mottled wind-blown texture. It is unlike any kind of rendering hitherto experienced in architecture and has the

c

curious quality of never appearing to set firm ('sticky rendering' might be a good name for it).

All renderings form a good base for colour-washing. Plain limewash has been used since the eleventh century when even the exteriors of large buildings such as castle towers were so treated, some degree of permanency being achieved by mixing tallow with the quicklime when it was being slaked with water. Such treatment was an excellent way of finishing rubble walling, but even the finely-wrought interior stonework of the cathedral was sometimes whitened, neat lines of imitation stone-work being subsequently drawn upon it with red paint. Many of the gleaming houses of the Regency owe their brilliance to an application of what was called 'lead oxide' to Roman cement rendering, while the cob wall of the seventeenth-century 'cottage' was often coloured pink to suggest brickwork.

These systems of facing and rendering are all connected with walling of stone and brick. Such walling could only have been constructed by masons—the 'nobblers' or rubble-masons who worked in field-stone, the freemasons who constructed true masonry, or the 'red masons' who raised walls of brick. Such work was extremely difficult to finance and its craftsmen not easily come by. The traditional house-builder of England was the carpenter, a man so skilled in his craft that today he would be called a joiner. For it was he who fashioned the systems of morticing by means of which he framed-up the house-walls of Englishmen of the later Middle Ages and the period of the Tudor monarchs.

Such building, too, was expensive and not for any but the most affluent of clients. Indeed, it should be emphasised that the timber building of, say, the fifteenth century, like that of previous centuries, was architecture in its highest form and employed only in the finest buildings. What we nowadays call a 'cottage' was most probably built originally as a home for a rich farmer, merchant or tradesman, while ordinary folk still lived in hovels they had to build themselves.

The half-timber houses so familiar today were built in what would seem to us a curious fashion—storey by storey, each formed of timber screens having vertical members or 'studs' set at top and bottom into 'heads' and 'sills'. The house plan was set out as a grid of strong posts, twelve to sixteen feet or so apart, arranged round the building in a rectangle having as its narrowest dimension the span of the house roof. The plan was divided longitudinally into a number of building bays indicated by opposing pairs of posts carrying a heavy beam or summer spanning across the house and carrying the joists of the upper floor (Fig 10). Between the posts the house-wrights set the framed screens they had been making from the smaller timbers collected for the house, the whole exterior of the house being built in this way, with occasionally a cross-screen acting as a partition between rooms.

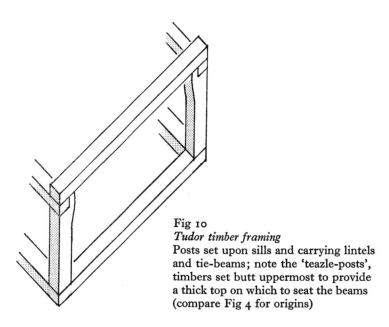

Fig 10
Tudor timber framing
Posts set upon sills and carrying lintels and tie-beams; note the 'teazle-posts', timbers set butt uppermost to provide a thick top on which to seat the beams (compare Fig 4 for origins)

The builders had discovered long ago that the feet of crucks or posts set in the ground soon rotted away, so, they were now mounting all their posts on heavy timber sills, these again being often set upon a plinth of field-stone to raise the perishable timber away from the damp ground. The ground sill of the building also acted as the support for the timbering of the screen walls of the ground storey.

This was the period when an upper floor or 'solar' (pronounced *soller*) was considered necessary as a sleeping area. The timber soller (so written during the Middle Ages) was carried by floor joists laid flat so as to give them a better setting upon the timber walls. It will be appreciated nowadays that joists laid this way were almost certain to sag when people walked upon them, but it was not until the end of the seventeenth century that this came to be understood by the English house-builder —which illustrates how strangely ignorant the builders of the Middle Ages and even later centuries were of the most elementary mechanics.

Not that a sagging floor would have mattered very much. But if an upper storey were added by setting it upon those floor joists, the movement of the floor would have caused the whole of the upper storey to jig about. This resulted in the discovery by the late-medieval builders that by projecting the ends of the floor-joists two feet or so beyond the ground storey and mounting the upper storey on the ends of these joists, the weight of the upper part of the building would stabilise the floor by acting as a counterpoise to the weight of persons moving about on it. This was the principle underlying the 'jetty' (Fig 11) which gives

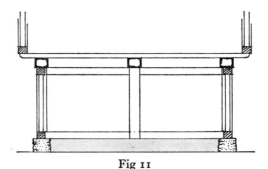

Fig 11
The jetty
Upper floor carried out over the lower
walling so that upper walling set upon it
can act as counterpoise to loads within
the storey

the characteristic top-heavy appearance to late-medieval and Tudor timber buildings. Any further upper storeys had to be constructed in the same fashion, so that tall buildings facing each other across a narrow city street would have their upper storeys almost touching each other.

At the head of each of the main posts at least two beams entered it. To take the mortices required for these beams without splitting the post the head of this was left thicker than the lower part. Such posts were usually set upside down with the root end providing the thickening; they were known as 'teazle-posts' (see Fig 10). The corner post was often elaborately carved; to tie it into the floor a 'dragon' (diagonal) beam was usually provided. In fine town houses of several storeys the mounting series of corner posts often forms an interesting architectural feature.

An enormous amount of good forest oak went into the construction of the houses of the fifteenth and sixteenth centuries. It is interesting to note that the timbers employed were seldom square in section, the longer side generally 2in more than the shorter. Large posts and beams were about 16in × 14in and floor joists and rafters perhaps 8in × 6in. Until the end of the seventeenth century beams were all laid 'flat' and posts were set—perhaps in memory of the early cruck, with the longest dimension at right angles to the span of the building. The whole structure was set up in the saw-pit, knocked apart and dragged to the site for re-erection. Everyone has noticed the joints marked with incised Roman numerals assisting this operation.

While the forests of England were being denuded in this fashion for building timber, even greater inroads were being made into them to provide fuel for the smelting of iron required by the great host of village smiths. During the reign of Elizabeth everyone could see the great trees falling and being dragged through the streets to be converted into homes, the construction of which employed so much closely spaced timbering that it could appear as if the house was being constructed almost of solid timber. It was not until the Armada scare of the 1580s that the Queen herself became concerned with the building

of warships and began to wonder whether her realm was working up to
a serious timber shortage. Hence we see at this time a noticeable change
in the design of the framed screen walls of the house of the period. The
closely spaced studs (Fig 12) ceased to appear and with them went the

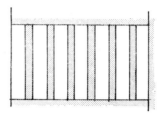

Fig 12
Early timber walling
'Studs' set close together between head and sill

ancient system of screen-making. Indeed no more individual screens
were constructed, the main posts of the building being joined by a
system of smaller beams and posts arranged to form much larger
panels, squarish in shape (Fig 13). In order to make up for the reduction

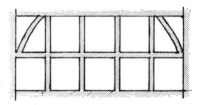

Fig 13
Later timber walling
From end of sixteenth century onwards a more
economical use of timber

in the timber content of the structure some slanting timbers called
braces were run here and there across the panels to introduce the
device known as triangulation which prevented the panels from becoming distorted. From experimenting with odd pieces of timber there

developed the elaborate system of timberwork which during the early seventeenth century covered such counties as Hereford, Cheshire and Shropshire, Worcestershire and Warwickshire with black-and-white 'magpie' houses having their structural panelling converted into elaborate Gothic forms. This style represented the final achievement of the English house-wright, but quite apart from this the square-panelled timber house continued to flourish until well into the eighteenth century.

The rapid spread of a fully developed style of timber architecture following the long period when the mason had ruled supreme is more easily appreciated when one considers not only the expense of masonry walling but the amount of space within the building it took up. One could not build a masonry wall less than thirty inches thick, whereas a perfectly sound and durable framed one could be reduced to about eight inches.

Within the early medieval house there were hardly any partitions as we know them today. With stone partitions impracticable for the reasons noted above, the interior of the house was originally either divided by hangings of tapestry or even sacking, or not at all. Not until the Gothic era do we find internal partitions formed of framed screens such as were later used to form the exteriors of the timber houses.

We have referred to the old 'brattices' formed of boards set on alternate sides of a screen to cover each other's spaces. In fine medieval buildings this device became transformed into an elaborate system of framing with one element converted into vertical bars and the other into an infilling of boards set between them. The moulded bars became 'mullions' like those in the Gothic windows; after the abbeys had been pulled down in 1539 the screen-makers brought their craft into the new houses of the period, replacing the mullions with flat timbers moulded along their edges and called 'muntins'. The houses of the early seventeenth century can show many such screens; they were developed by the introduction of horizontal rails to form systems of square panels.

One of the simplest ways of building employed during the early Middle Ages for quite large, if only semi-permanent, houses such as rural farmhouses had been to develop the tan system of construction by surrounding the house with poles set close together in the ground and joined together by a system of woven 'wattling' formed of willow wands woven from pole to pole. On this framework an adequate if not very permanent wall could be fashioned by daubing it with clay. When the timber-framed screen replaced the wall of poles, the wattle-and-daub was used for filling in the panels of the screenwork, the sides of the vertical 'studs' being grooved to take the wattling in the same fashion as the surrounds of a window were grooved to take the glazing (see Fig 14).

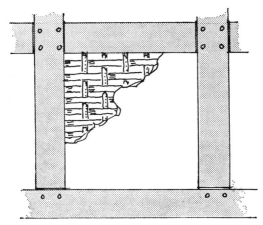

Fig 14
Wattle-and-daub
Panels of timbering
filled with wattling of
hazel, willow, etc and
daubed with clay or cob

Another way of filling the panels of the timber-framed house was to wall them up with pieces of stone or brick set in mortar. When whole bricks were used they were often set 'herring-bone' fashion to wedge them in more tightly, but ordinary coursed brickwork was commonly used in the large panels of the seventeenth century. The filling of a timber frame is known as nogging.

The trouble with all framed timberwork is that the movement of the timber, expecially while it is 'seasoning', can result in the opening of the joints between it and the nogging to produce so many leaks that the only really satisfactory way of keeping the house watertight is by cladding it with some outer sheath.

The more important buildings of the Anglo-Saxon era and the early Middle Ages had their timberwork completely sheathed with shingles made of short oak boards overlapping in courses, as we see in tile-hanging today. Each course 'broke joint' with its neighbour, so that each shingle covered the joint in the course below. To make their water-shedding more efficient the bottom edge of each shingle was rounded off, giving the building an appearance of being covered with fish-scales. Shingles without this embellishment may still be seen on small church steeples; the fish-scale type has been reproduced in tile-hanging.

Shingles being an impermanent material we do not know how long they were used for sheathing. Their use for roofing began to decline early in the Middle Ages when sheets of lead became the universal covering for the roofs of important buildings, but they may well have remained in use for sheathing timber-framed buildings to a later period than we yet have evidence for.

Stone tiles have been in use since medieval days for roofing important buildings. In some special areas, notably the Cotswolds and Sussex, beds of limestone exist which when quarried into lumps and left on edge in frosty weather will split into tiles suitable for covering roofs. These were the medieval tiles, laid by the 'tylers' of the day, which replaced the shingles with a permanent substitute. Some of these stone tiles are very heavy; they vary considerably in size and are laid in graduating courses with the larger tiles nearest the eaves so as to lessen the load higher up the roof.

In some regions of England one may find very special quarries from which roofing slate may be obtained. Cornwall and Westmorland produce beautiful slates. South Devon used to produce slates which were not only used for roofing buildings but for sheathing them as well. Some of the hanging slates were shaped in similar fashion to the old shingles.

When bricks began to appear for general use in walling, clay tiles for roof coverings were not slow in following them. They were hung by driving wooden pegs through them in the same way as for the earlier stone tiles and shingles. During the last century, when machine-made tiles began to come into use, these had little projecting 'nibs' cast on to them for hanging over the roofing battens.

England has always been a timber-building country, the timber used being native oak. But towards the end of the eighteenth century foreign softwood, mainly pine, was imported for making the frames of cheap houses and covering them with the overlapping boarding known as weatherboarding. Softwood had never been used externally before and it was soon discovered that it would not stand up to the English climate. To protect the wood it was covered with what was called 'lead oxide' which was in fact white paint. A crop of white weatherboarded houses began to appear on the east side of England, the small houses of the Regency which later went to America and developed Classical detail to create the graceful 'Colonial' style of architecture.

Once white-painted weatherboarding had been adopted as a sheathing for framed walls it was used as an alternative to clay tiles for covering the leaky panels of the old timber-framed houses, many of which have now been covered up so that their old framing no longer shows. As fast as the pine 'deals' came into the ports, so fast did the 'lead oxide' factories spring up all along the Thames estuary to produce the essential paint for covering the weatherboarding.

Thus was discovered the use of paint to brighten the house-front. Much of the Roman cement rendering also came to be painted white, completely changing the face of the countryside which had hitherto produced houses of stone and brick and oak but was now a land gleaming with white paint. Brown pigment was added to the paint if one wanted a pine beam to look like oak. But the decoratively coloured house-paint of today did not appear until the middle of the nineteenth century.

An interesting variation of the principle of waterproofing by weatherboard sheathing may be seen at the seaside where one may find old houses tarred as though they were the hulls of boats. The best-quality boarding was smoothly finished, with notches cut along the underside of each board to enable it to cover the edge of the board below it, and a bevel run along the exposed edge to soften its appearance. This is sometimes known as 'clapboard'. Weatherboard of good quality is only used today in connection with traditional architecture, but a cheap variety made of fir, with 'waney' edges, is sometimes seen; it is usually creosoted. It will be appreciated that any kind of weatherboarding has to be fastened to the framing behind it with a great number of nails and that it was not until these could be machine-made in quantity that the system could be employed. Thus weatherboarding is essentially a product of the Industrial Revolution.

The 'contemporary' buildings of today depart far more drastically from traditional building systems. But after their own fashion they are as illustrative of their particular structural arrangement as the buildings of the Tudor period. They are what is known as functionalist in that they display the building structure without any consideration for aesthetic refinements. The style is sometimes called 'functionalistic architecture' but the term is a misnomer as the term 'functionalist' is by derivation a negation of architecture as it has been understood down the centuries when the skill of the craftsman was employed to endow every building with aesthetic appeal.

The frame of the functionalist building is similar in principle to that of the timber-framed buildings of past centuries but instead of timber posts and beams we have 'stanchions' or pillars and beams of steel or reinforced concrete.

Owing to the far greater strength of the modern material, the building bays in which the structure is set out are much larger than of old and the filling of the panels requires a different approach. Generally a light steel frame is used, divided up into its own panels, the upper portion filled with glass and the lower portion with steel painted for protection. Alternatively the frame can be mounted upon a low wall of block construction serving as a parapet to the concrete floor.

Light steel frames holding a filling of panels of glass or sheet steel are known today as 'curtain walling'—a sad misnomer when one remembers that the original use of the term was to designate the lofty perimeter of the medieval castle.

The latest stage in building technique is to cover the whole of the structural framework with a vast sheet of 'curtain walling'—a strange development from functionalism which at least presented the building's structure. This style of completely sheathed building seems to represent the ultimate in the downward trend of architecture in that no recognisable design of any sort can be detected and the whole is just a sheer wall of glass and steel sheet.

Buildings of this sort are completed at their summits by roofs which are simply repetitions of the reinforced concrete floors within, sealed over with some waterproofing material such as asphalt. These anonymous hidden roofs have travelled far from the ancient ones which were not only the glory of the building but originally may have formed the whole of it, as in the case of the house built on crucks. And asphalt seems very far removed indeed from the thatch of old times.

Roofing timbers in those days were joined together by rough poles called spars—precursors of the battens of the days of tiling—between which was stuffed the thatching material—fern, heather, furze, or, in the best examples, straw or reed tied to them in bundles by strips of hazel. During long centuries the house-builders of England learnt all there was to know about thatch. Just as it was difficult to build the angles of an early building in field-stone, so was it awkward to try to make thatch adopt a rectangular form. There were no gable-ends to early thatched buildings, their corners being swept round and the thatch over curved in sympathy, so that the whole looked like one of those haystacks now almost banished from the countryside by the baler.

The angle of pitch of thatch was 50–55 degrees, steep enough to throw off snow but not so steep as to offer too much resistance to wind. Even a steep roof, however, provides little interior headroom if one stands close to the eaves, so the house-room was made as long as possible by pitching the end slopes of the roof so steep that they were not far removed from being gables (Fig 15). Later, when thatching materials improved and the technique of the craft improved, rectangular houses could be given proper gabled ends with the thatch coming out over them in the manner of 'verges' (see Fig 17). A change to shingles, which are difficult to sweep round curves, might also have

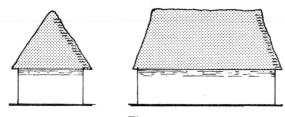

Fig 15
Early form of thatching
Thatch carried all round building; ends steeper than
sides to assist headroom

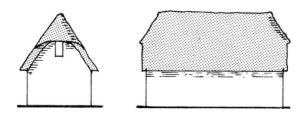

Fig 16
Semi-gable
End wall part raised to give room for attic window;
thatch continued over as 'Sussex hip'

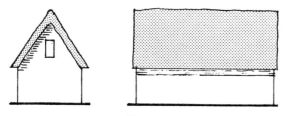

Fig 17
Gabled house
Complete gables raised at either end of house and
thatch carried complete from end to end

led to the rebuilding of the ends of the house; during the Middle Ages one frequently reads of instructions to provide a house with a gable.

The weight of roof-covering—and thatch is enormously heavy—tends to make the roof subside until the feet of the rafters spread and begin to slide off the wall-tops. Hence it was invariably the custom to provide each pair of rafters with a 'collar', tying them together at about head-height.

With the framed timber wall coming in at the end of the medieval period, the south-east of England introduced a compromise form of house end by raising the timber frame as far as the roof-collars and then continuing upwards and back as a pitched roof. This enabled a window for lighting the attic to be introduced at the end of the house. Roofs which sweep round the end of a house instead of ending at the verges of a gable are known as hipped roofs; the small hipped end set above an incomplete gable is known as a Sussex hip (Fig 16).

When clay tiles came into use and roofs could not change pitch at the angles without breaking the courses of tiles, the completely 'hipped' roof (see Fig 24) designed as part of the building, became universally employed. Such roofs were mitred at the angles, hip rafters carrying the short jack rafters introduced at the angles of the roof to carry the battens round them.

The exterior walling of English houses, especially those built of framed or cob construction, must be protected from the roof-water which might run down them by projecting the roof as eaves. Heavy thatch, perhaps two feet in thickness, always projects well forward of the wall-face. During a storm, the stormwater sweeps forcibly off the roof, hastened by its steep pitch, but all roofs drip long after the storm has ended so that gutters set in the ground are often provided to collect these drips. There are also eaves gutters, originally formed of boards set at an angle and supported upon smith-wrought brackets—as they used to spout their stormwater out at the ends they are often known as spoutings.

The house-wrights of Britain having always been a highly skilled body of men—the Anglo-Saxon word for 'to build' was the same as for 'to timber'—one can appreciate that the ramifications and development of their craft would make a life-time's study. We know enough about the roof-building—and steeple-building—exploits of the Anglo-Saxons to be able to realise that they achieved a technique which, though vanished alas with the great architectural style which it created, in its day achieved tremendous feats of joinery. It was the inevitable changeover from timber-building to masonry which during the eleventh century raised the master-mason to be the architect in place of the master-wright.

The change was revolutionary, for what really happened was that posted construction vanished almost completely for centuries, only being re-established with the dynasty of the Tudor monarchs. The masonry wall had now arrived, and the carpenter's contribution was restricted to covering this with a roof. These roofs were of the simplest, almost primitive, construction, consisting of pairs of rafters set against each other across the building and joined together with timber collars (see Fig 18). From the eleventh to the sixteenth century these 'couples'

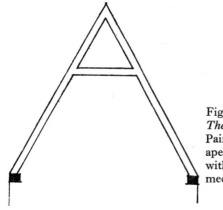

Fig 18
The 'couple'
Pairs of rafters pinned together at apex and tied together near this with 'collar'. Universal form of medieval roof

were set in their thousands over the houses of tgnıs
made presents of couples cut from royal forests. A roof simply consisting of lines of couples set about 2ft apart—a type of roof still in use

today—is still known as close-couple. In large-span buildings such as
cathedrals very long rafters had to be used and the collars reinforced
and stiffened with systems of timber struts and braces but the close-
couple principle remained the same.

As an example of roof-construction the medieval couple was woefully
unsound when set upon walling, as the tendency of the rafter feet to
spread under the weight of the roof covering either caused them to
slip off the wall-tops or, if securely fixed there, simply to topple the
whole wall over (as can be seen today in many an old village church).

The obvious remedy for this would have been to tie together the
rafter-feet, or even the wall-tops, with what we call today a tie-beam.
But this would have been a device utterly unacceptable to the medieval
house-owner. The ancient hall had been designed since Anglo-Saxon
times to create the effect of a great vaulted cavern and the introduction

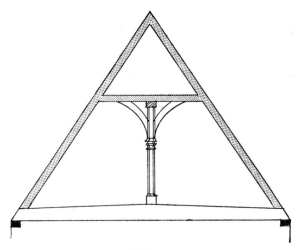

Fig 19
Tie-beam and king-post
The feet of the rafters are tied with a cross-beam upon
which is mounted a king-post in its turn supporting a
longitudinal beam passing beneath the collars and
preventing them from settling

of a tie-beam crossing this space would have constituted an affront to the dignity of the medieval noble—as bad as putting in an iron tie-rod today. Even his chamber roof could not have been permitted to display such an ugly structural device.

With the reintroduction of posted construction, however, in which two posts joined together by a tie-beam formed a basic element in the structure, it was not so easy to be indignant about the intrusive timber. It was, in fact, made use of to carry a short post, which in its turn supported a longitudinal beam called a 'purlin' passing beneath the collars of the roof-couples. This ingenious device effectively checked any tendency of the roof to subside. The 'king-post', so frequently discovered in fifteenth- and sixteenth-century house-roofs, is usually developed into a charming little colonnette with moulded base and cap from which curved struts sweep up to collars and purlins (Fig 19).

But this structural system based upon a tie-beam could not have been accepted in an exposed roof intended to be seen from below as an architectural feature of the house. The Gothic carpenters dealt with this problem by constructing a heavy arch of timber in place of a tie-beam and carrying the king-post on the crown of the arch (Fig 20). It is fine arches of this type which provide the principal architectural features of the halls of the Tudor yeomen and are also seen in the roofs of their bedchambers. Today the arches and their attendant king-posts are often lost to view among the water-tanks of an attic.

Another attractive feature of the Tudor roof appears with the introduction of side-purlins instead of the single one carrying the collar. These purlins are often supported by small curved struts called wind-braces which pass along the underside of the roof in the fashion of an arcade. The introduction of the side-purlin indicates the abandoning of the ancient roofing-couple in favour of separate rafters carried by a series of purlins in the fashion followed today.

The use of the tie-beam to help in carrying the Tudor roof led to this becoming the basis of what is known as a roofing truss, that is to say a triangular frame of heavy principal rafters resting on the tie-beam and carrying side-purlins passing longitudinally along the roof and

D

carrying the common rafters directly, instead of through the medium of collars. Thereafter the roof-truss or principal becomes the basis of the house-roof and spells the end of the medieval couple.

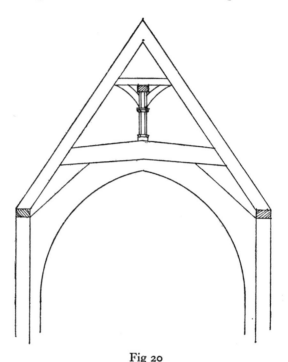

Fig 20
Arched truss
In the timber hall of the Tudor yeoman the obtrusive tie-beam was replaced by a heavy timber arch carrying the king-post and framed up with heavy 'principal rafters' to form the first complete roof-truss

Substitution of an attractive but structurally unsound timber arch for an efficient tie-beam weakened the stability of a roof considerably, and such arches were used sparingly. The yeoman's hall of the Tudor era was usually about twenty feet wide and thirty long. A single arch spanned it, the ends of the hall being formed of framed partitions which were in fact the side walls of the cross-chambers and served as gable walls for the ends of the hall.

Conversion during the Elizabethan era of the roof-space into living accommodation put an end to arched trusses, as the crown of the arch projected into this. A simple truss based on a tie-beam took its place. But as a king-post would have obstructed a central passage along the attic space, a new type of truss was devised, called a queen-post truss, having a pair of posts instead of a single one (Fig 21). Thenceforth, until the coming of the Renaissance roof towards the end of the seventeenth century, the queen-post truss forms the basis of most house-roofs. Curved struts were often set from the bottom of the posts to the sides of the truss. In the barn roofs of the seventeenth century the posts are often omitted and only the struts remain.

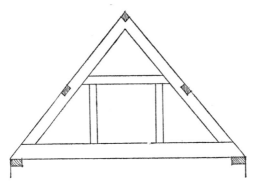

Fig 21
Queen-post truss
The Elizabethan truss with tie-beam, principal
rafters, collar, and a pair of queen-posts which
may be vertical or curved outwards. Longitudinal purlins are led from truss to truss to
carry the rafters

During the Middle Ages all buildings were of single-span type, which means that they were never set side by side with a common roof covering both. Additions to such buildings had to be made by building

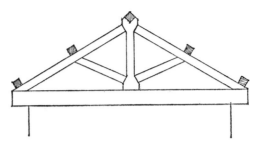

Fig 22
Renaissance truss
Tie-beam, principal rafters, king-post and
struts scientifically framed together. The
truss is still used today

at right angles, either as a projecting wing or as a cross-chamber, for
setting two single-span buildings side by side would leave a trough
between their roofs (see Fig 48a) in which snow would collect and
cause water to soak into the building. Lateral expansion had therefore
to be achieved by continuing one of the roof-slopes downwards in a
'catslide'—the system adopted in adding aisles to an early church nave.
In a house such appendages are known as outshots (see Fig 23).

After the suppression of the abbeys very large amounts of lead were
lifted from the vast roofs of deserted churches, and their erstwhile
maintenance plumbers employed in constructing valley gutters between
roofs which were now being set side by side. Thus the old straggling
medieval house began to disappear and the house plan assembled into
something more nearly a square.

With the introduction of the Renaissance movement at the beginning
of the seventeenth century the tall old medieval roofs began to disappear,
roofs of a very much flatter pitch becoming the fashion now that they
could be covered with sheets of lead. In small houses, clay tiles began
to come into use, bringing down roof pitches to as low as 40 degrees,
while at the end of the eighteenth century the use of close-fitting
slates brought from North Wales by the new canals enabled roof
pitches to be reduced by yet another 10 degrees.

The Renaissance roof was now established. Its truss can be easily recognised. Low in pitch, it is formed of four principal members—the horizontal tie-beam, the raking rafters, and the sturdy king-post in no way resembling the charming feature seen in the fifteenth-century roof but possibly perpetuating its memory. From its foot to the mid-point of each rafter is a plain strut (Fig 22).

In the larger houses of the seventeenth century the little 'Sussex hip' (Fig 16) came to be expanded to cover the whole of the end of the house with a complete hipped end (Fig 24). This type of roof was most useful when roofing a square double-span house such as was being built for the late seventeenth-century squire (Fig 24).

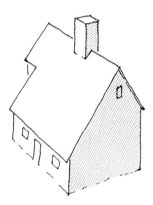

Fig 23
The outshot
Single-storey annexe covered
by the main roof projected
downwards

At this period an interesting form of roof covering was to be seen in East Anglia. This was the curly pantile—a development of the ancient Roman tiling system perpetuated in Spain to this day—brought over from the Spanish Netherlands to cover almost all the long farmhouses of the eastern side of England. The pantile cannot be made to turn corners, so East Anglian houses all end in gables. The same applied to Welsh slates when they appeared, thus hipped ends disappeared from the houses of the Regency, and low gables, often containing a charming little window, are found instead.

A curious form of roof appears during this period. Named after the French architect Mansart, the very large mansard roof accommodates the whole of the upper storey of the building between very steeply pitched slopes, above which the roof subsides to a normal pitch (Fig 25).

Common to the nineteenth century is the outshot. The employment of Welsh slates kept its roof pitch down so that it no longer had to rely for covering upon the prolongation of the main roof into a catslide.

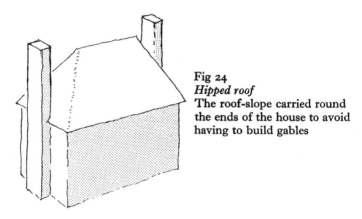

Fig 24
Hipped roof
The roof-slope carried round the ends of the house to avoid having to build gables

A simple form of roof once only used to cover 'linhays' for housing farm carts is the monopitch, which is simply a lean-to with nothing to lean against. It is popular today among 'avant-garde' architects.

During the wool-rich fifteenth century, when parish churches throughout England were being rebuilt in stately fashion, their roofs were being covered with lead sheets laid so skilfully that the pitch of the roof could be kept down almost to the horizontal. In the next century, after the lead of the abbey churches had been transferred to domestic uses, the craft of the plumber had so far developed that only a token fall was needed.

Lead roofs do not project beyond the wall-faces as eaves but have to be stopped at a parapet behind which is a square box-gutter formed in the lead (Fig 26), water from this being allowed to spout out through stone gargoyles. From Tudor times onwards the stormwater from the parapet gutters was led into down-spouts passing down the walls and discharging into ground-gutters at their foot.

Fig 25
Mansard roof
Of French origin (architect
Mansart); includes the whole
of the top storey within it

The next development, only applicable to tiled roofs, was a return
to projecting eaves and the provision of eaves-gutters, lead troughs
carried by smith-wrought iron brackets secured to the wall-face
below and accompanied by square lead down-spouts. At best, eaves-
gutters are fragile features and the weight of the lead soon became too
much for rusted iron; thus few old eaves-gutters have survived to this
day. Their successors are the cast-iron rainwater goods of today which
unless they are kept painted inside and out are even more ephemeral
than their lead ancestors.

Fig 26
Parapet gutter
Where a parapet was desired
instead of projecting eaves, a
lead gutter had to be formed
behind it and the stormwater
discharged through spoutings

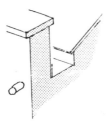

Thatch as a roof covering has been mentioned. Straw thatch is laid
in two styles the most efficient of which is known as reed thatching
even though the material be straw reed. In reed thatching the straw is
laid almost horizontally. In 'long-straw' thatching it is laid at a steeper
angle and does not hold so securely, being in reality intended only for
the short-lived thatches once seen on ricks.

Clay roofing tiles are always slightly curved downwards to make their lower edges grip the tiles below. Large tiles, called tile-and-a-half, are used to strengthen the verges round gables. In first-class work the 'valleys' of the roof are 'swept', the courses of tiles being curved up and 'laced' together as they were originally. In cheaper work the valleys may be worked in lead, but special tiles are made for the purpose, as are bonnet tiles for hipped angles. Half-round ridge-tiles are normal but parabolic ones look much neater. Tudor ridge-tiles often survive the re-roofing of old houses; they have their crests pinched into coxcombs and, surprisingly, may sometimes be found mixed with modern ones along the ridge of an old roof (Fig 27).

Fig 27
Tudor ridge-tile
A number of these have survived
centuries of re-roofing

The great delight of a roof of clay tiles is the way in which it collects lichens and acquires a patina. This can never heppen with tiles made of concrete so that roofs so covered always look dull and lifeless. A way to instil a little vitality into a roof of concrete tiles is to mix two or three closely associated tones and scatter them over the slopes. The sombre slates of North Wales and the lovely slates of Cornwall and Westmorland have been discussed earlier, and of course the ancient stone tiles of the Cotswold houses.

Flat roofs are laid on boarding nailed not to rafters but to roofing joists laid like floor joists across from wall to wall. Now that lead roofing has become so expensive an impermanent substitute has been devised, consisting of felt-based tarred sheeting laid in several strata and afterwards sealed with tar and small stone-chippings.

After the provision of a waterproof roof had been accorded the primitive Englishman, his next necessity was a fire-hearth. The hearth itself presented no problem, a small paved arc serving this purpose. The problem was the disposal of smoke, any provision for which meant a breach in the defences of the house. The simplest method was to allow the smoke to accumulate high up in the roof and provide a small hole somewhere through which it might be sucked by an accommodating wind. Gableless houses thatched all round became 'black houses', such as remain today in parts of Scotland. We are told that a barrel with its ends knocked out might provide a primitive chimney to a peasant's cot.

During the eleventh century when important houses and castle towers had their bedchambers on upper floors a central hearth could not be provided. Proper fireplaces were, however, formed in the thick stone walling and apertures provided above and behind the cavernous embrasures to let the smoke escape. Fireplaces continued to be used in upper chambers throughout the Middle Ages.

In small houses the obstructive position of the central hearth led to its being moved to one side of the main room and set against a reredos of stone (Fig 28), further protection to the house walls being provided by the erection of 'cheeks' on either side of the hearth. The smoke from the reredos still drifted up towards the ridge. But if an upper floor should be required this formed an obstruction to the smoke and some other provision for it had to be devised. When chimney flues or tunnels began

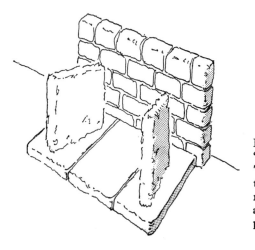

Fig 28
'Reredos'
The central fire-hearth transferred to the side of the room. When set into the wall and arched over it becomes a proper fireplace with a flue

to be constructed over the arched embrasures of medieval fireplaces one inevitable problem presented itself, for the prolongation of the tunnel above the eaves of the roof created a valley at this point, trapping snow and rainwater from the roof slopes and allowing damp to seep into the house. A way of dealing with this problem was to fill in between the chimney and the roof with a small lateral roof, like that over a dormer window, impinging against the back of the stack (Fig 29a). This obviated the necessity for calling in a plumber to construct a chimney gutter. In order to escape the problem altogether some builders set

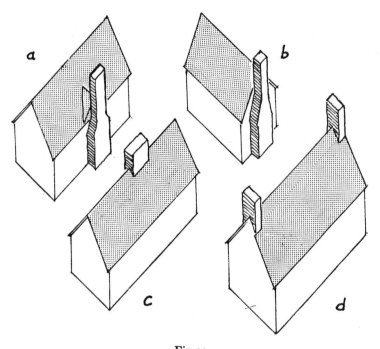

Fig 29
Positions of chimneys
(a) Normal medieval position (note special provision required for shedding snow from behind it), (b) alternative position to obviate this problem, (c) seventeenth-century central stack, (d) eighteenth-century (and later) pairs of end-stacks

their fireplaces in the end walls of chambers so that the chimney could be incorporated with the gable wall (Fig 29b). In the ground-floor apartments of the day, however, it was customary to set the hearth in the side wall of the room where it distributed its heat more efficiently. As one faces a manor house of the early seventeenth century one can usually see the chimney stacks of hall and parlour rising behind the roof.

Towards the end of the previous century, the distribution of the abbey lands had set the new grantees a housing problem as they attempted to settle in their tenants. This resulted in a new type of standard house plan being developed which provided for a central chimney stack serving both rooms; this will be discussed later. Once this central stack had appeared (see Fig 29c), forests of them began to arise, to the wonder of the Elizabethan chronicler William Harrison, until the tall central stack became the sign-manual of the seventeenth-century farmhouse.

These stacks, however, proved troublesome obstructions to the accommodation within the house, and during the eighteenth century they disappeared, split up into a pair of stacks passing up each gable and creating the characteristic silhouette of the Georgian roof-top (Fig 29d). In these lateral positions the chimney stacks remained throughout the Victorian era.

In its defence against the English winter the house's weakest spot was its entrance doorway. Except in farmhouses, where the entrance was shared by the farmer and his animals until the architectural revolution at the end of the sixteenth century, doorways were kept narrow and low. Wherever possible some kind of screen was interposed between the entrance doorway and the living room into which it led. A short projecting spur was often provided (Fig 30). In the long farmhouses, however, complete screens reached right across the building, flanking an entrance passage which provided an excellent inner porch (see Figs 34, 35 and 43). By the end of the sixteenth century these screens often became good examples of the screen-maker's craft, transferred to the house from the lost churches of the monks.

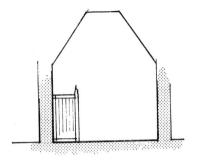

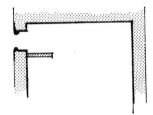

Fig 30
'Spur' screen
Short length of screen set inside
outer door to deflect draughts
from dais

An external porch was a great asset to the comfort of the house in that
it assisted the interior spur in sheltering the living room from draughts.
Some of the most primitive of the early farmhouses were provided with
some kind of porch, but the house-porch proper does not appear until
dignity had been achieved, with the ejection of the cattle to their own
quarters in the farmyard.

The two-storeyed 'King John's houses' of the twelfth century (see
Fig 36) were always entered on the upper floor, the ground storey, used
only for storage, being entered from the floor above. Wide stone stairs
led up to the entrance doorway. The internal stair was often a circular
'vice' fitted into an angle.

When the house-owner began to provide himself with a chamber
floor by setting boards across the roof-ties—which was not until he had
solved the smoke problem by building a fireplace with a chimney—he
reached this up a ladder fixed to the walls, as may be seen to this day
in early cottages. The new houses of the late sixteenth-century housing

boom were provided with wooden spiral stairs, copied from the stone vices of church towers, set against their great chimney stacks. Many of them remain today—their sites are also frequently indicated by a tiny staircase window, little more than a slit.

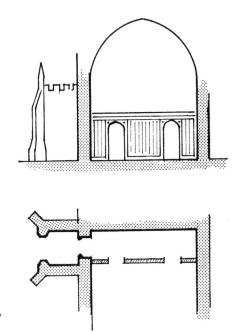

Fig 31
Hall screen
Complete screen crossing end of medieval hall and forming passage known as 'the screens'

The great Elizabethan mansions had straight flights of stairs built by the carpenters in imitation of the external stairs built by the masons. As is usual in timber architecture, they were beautifully joinered, balustraded, and enriched with carving as they passed up the walls of the stair-halls specially planned for them. They were the ancestors of a great variety of grand stairways curving round the halls of Georgian and later days.

When at last the great central chimney stack had been moved from the heart of the seventeenth-century house, its place was usually taken by a 'pair of stairs' rising to and from a half-landing (Fig 32). These 'dog-leg' stairs first appeared in the terrace houses built in the suburbs of London by speculative builders of the Commonwealth period. Thenceforth they became universal features of terrace planning and of course remain with us to this day.

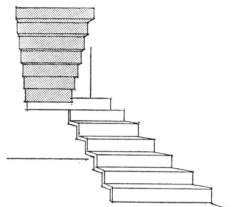

Fig 32
'Dog-leg' stairs
Devised during the Commonwealth; to become the universal stair of the future

Early medieval floors were formed of very heavy boarding up to six inches thick. Timber floors were virtually unknown to the early medieval builder. The first upper floors were the tops of vaulted undercrofts such as could have been seen beneath the dormitory of an abbey. When the stone soller came to be constructed with boarding on timber beams, this was only regarded as a foundation for an earthen floor such as existed below it, the boarding actually being covered with six inches or so of earth. It is possible that the manners of the period would have made boarded floors unsuitable; it was perhaps not until Tudor times that they became accepted as normal features in timber-framed houses.

Floor joists were about eight inches by six and set about eight inches apart. The maximum carry of these was about ten feet; thus either a longitudinal beam had to be carried on posts down the centre of the building, or this had to be divided into building bays by transverse beams known as summers—the word derived from the Old French *somier*, packhorse. All beams and joists were of course set flat.

The Elizabethans tried to combine the two systems of planning the summers so as to make them cross in the centre of the room to produce a cruciform arrangement in the ceiling. But morticing the centre of the main beam at its weakest point to take the longitudinal ones frequently caused the former to crack. It is a feature of Elizabethan houses that more often than not the main floor beams have been repaired with smith-made straps.

The Elizabethan use of attics set them to tidying up the roof timbers, which they did by morticing the purlins into the principal rafters instead of setting them one upon the other in a normal fashion. The result was the broken rafters one sees today in seventeenth-century roofs.

Breaches through their house walls were not popular with early house-owners, so windows were kept small, allowing only enough light to move about by. The early windows were just square holes, filled with a lattice of withies (Fig 33) and often barred as well. Shutters were usual—King Harold's last stand at Hastings was behind a shield wall made of shutters wrenched from the windows of nearby farmhouses.

Fig 33
Lattice window
Early window frame filled with lattice of laths; pattern eventually copied in lead-glazing

Medieval glass was made by spinning from a blow-pipe, 'quarries' some twelve square inches in size being cut from around the 'bullion' in the middle to which the pipe had been affixed. This centre piece— the fashionable bottle glass of today—would have been sold to the farmer at cut-price rates. The little quarries, fashioned into diamond-shapes to imitate the openings in the lattices, were gathered together into sheets by means of lead strips called 'calms'—pronounced 'cames'—the leadwork of the farmer's casement being probably fashioned out of scraps gathered in the ruins of some nearby abbey. The casements themselves were rectangular frames, wrought by the village smith, to which the glazed panels were secured by pieces of wire. The iron casements were hung on 'hooks and bands', the fretted 'cockspur' latches by which they were secured remain delightful features of seventeenth-century fenestration.

The fitting of an iron casement to a timber frame was fairly draught-proof, that to stone walling not at all. So the carpenters began to make frames of wood to insert into the window openings and take the iron frames of casements, both fixed and opening. Once the carpenter—now of course recognised as a 'joiner'—began to interest himself in the fenestration of a house it was but a short step to the complete replacement of the smith-wrought casement by the joinered cottage window used today.

Some of the wildest of the English winter weather may be encountered in the south-western counties of England. It was in these regions, towards the end of the seventeenth century, that an entirely new kind of window began to appear, spreading throughout the region, possibly from the great port of Plymouth. It was called the sash window—from the French word *chassis*—and its wooden sashes slid sideways along grooves cut in the head and sill of the window frame. It required no stays to hold it open against a wind that might well smash a casement, and fitted snugly in its grooves when closed.

From the horizontally sliding sash developed the hung sash which slid up and down in grooves provided in the sides of the window frame, a form of window ideally suited to the tall windows of the Renaissance buildings of the period. The earliest of these sashes had one half fixed and the other opening, but by the end of the seventeenth century both halves of the window were opening—as a double-hung sash window.

By the time the sash window had arrived the panes of glass had increased in size and pieces of up to a hundred square inches could be obtained. The sashes were now being provided with a grid of narrow bars called glazing bars, the whole system of sash and bars being grooved to take the glass. It is the pattern of these white-painted grids of glazing bars against a dark window opening which supplied much of the appeal of the Georgian house-front. But after the Industrial Revolution, the new rolling mills were able to produce far larger sheets of glass and the pattern of the glazing bars was seen no more in the double-hung sashes.

Still later we have the introduction of plate glass for the Victorian shop window.

Today we have the great gashes of the 'landscape' windows, mocking the taste of our ancestors who liked to keep their homes warm, cosy and private.

CHAPTER TWO

THE HOUSE PLAN

ANYONE WHO owns an old house, or visits one, or even notices one by
the roadside, may well discover that he would like to know more about
it: its age perhaps, its original form, the part it played in history.

The arrangement of accommodation in a house is called by architects
its plan. But when one is looking at a plan one should be able to appreciate just what it represents. The architect's drawing board notwithstanding, a plan represents nothing more than the first trace of the
house upon the ground and the last souvenir of it after it has been
pulled down.

The writer always feels sympathetic with a client who with furrowed
brow studies the plan of his new house while clearly wondering just
what it represents. For when looking at a plan the client has to try to
raise the walls to form a room, *raise* the door openings until they become
visually doorways, and *lift* the symbols indicating windows away from
the floor to try to see them for what in the eyes of the architect is quite
a simple feature.

In the same way, plans drawn by archaeologists from excavated
foundations mean very little to the layman—and for that matter, often
to the archaeologist himself unless he should be a trained architect. And
we can visualise little of a great cathedral from the plan in the guide
book, which is in reality merely a route-map.

It is the third dimension, the vertical, which when invoked raises the
building from a plan to architecture.

So it is to be hoped that anyone trying to read the plans in this book will try not to pass them over as linear designs but strive to raise the spaces between the walls to form rooms covered by a roof.

In the early days England had circular houses, called nowadays—offensively—huts. There were also rectangular houses, some of them of considerable size, but all perished long ago. The first large rectangular houses were those of farmers who kept their animals under the same roof as themselves so as to be able to watch over them at night.

The long axis of the farmhouse always sloped slightly, so that the floor of the building could be drained if flooded by stormwater and the living part kept free from the urine of the animals. It is this primitive requirement which has bestowed on the English house plan two definite and inescapable ends—the upper and the lower—with the farmer at the upper end and his cattle at the lower (see Fig 34).

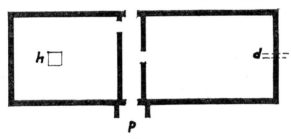

Fig 34
Primitive farmhouse
Set on a slope with a drain (d) leading away
from the part of the house occupied by the
cattle, the family living in the upper end
round the hearth (h); a porch (p) usually
provided

These early houses were simply very long rooms, set athwart the contour. Entered at the middle of a long wall, light screens separated the family from the small cattle of the day. The family end of the house was the site of the fire-hearth upon which cooking had to be done, at least in bad weather. Thus the living room—the 'house-place'—was in fact the farmhouse kitchen; for convenience, however, the main room in the house will be referred to as the living room.

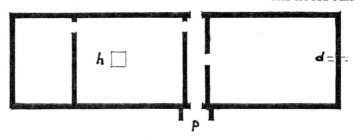

Fig 35
Developed farmhouse
An extra room appears at the upper end of the
living room which may be a retiring room or
'parlour', eventually becoming an essential
feature of the farmhouse plan

The hugger-mugger in a room in which all the humans—and probably
a few dogs as well—lived, cooked, ate and slept, can only be imagined by
comparison with, say, a Kaffir kraal, an Indian tepee, or an igloo, in all
of which the same conditions may well have obtained. So it is not
surprising that, perhaps during the expansive days of the twelfth
century, there was a tendency to add on to the upper end of the house
a small room whose purpose is not always certain, but which one
could easily imagine to be a private retreat for the house-owner. What
we can be sure of is that eventually, after the days of the poles-and-
wattle houses, and even those of early medieval times, this extra upper-
end room became the parlour—the place where one could hear one's
own voice!

By the end of the sixteenth century, by which time the cattle had
been finally turned out of the house into their own byres and shippons,
we can see the house plan quite definitely established as the upper
part of the old long house with its subdivision into kitchen and parlour
(Fig 44).

But this is taking us too far ahead, for house architecture on a far less
primitive scale had been progressing through five centuries before this.
The great hall of the Anglo-Saxon and Norman magnates had been
developing along its own quite different lines. And, moreover, an

entirely novel kind of house had been appearing in scores throughout the country, the stone-built dormitories of the monks, two-storeyed above a vaulted undercroft.

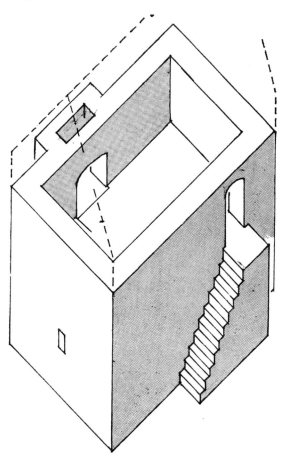

Fig 36
A King John's house
The first stone-built private house appears towards end of twelfth century. A 'chamber' with fireplace raised above a storage basement. Only approach is up an external stair

These monastic houses represented a complete revolution in the English way of life, for this had hitherto proceeded entirely at ground level. It was the influence of the Byzantines, who in the centuries immediately preceding the Norman invasion had ordered European civilisation, which had set the bedchambers of the rich *above*, and not beside, their animals.

Diminutives of the great house of the monks—today called King John's houses—were built for the occupation of the lords of the great halls. As well as having the advantage of an elevated bedchamber, these houses provided a basement for the storage of valuables including the money chest (see Fig 36). During the twelfth century the term 'house'—sometimes even called 'chamber' in consideration of its principal apartment—referred to one of these small stone dwellings. A royal palace comprised a great hall with its array of offices surrounded by the actual residences, a collection of houses—for the king, the queen, the royal children, the chancellor and other important officials—all of the type described above. Access from many of these to the hall-door was under covered ways. It was from such pentices in monasteries that the cloister developed.

Eventually a small stone house came to be added at the upper end of the nobleman's hall itself so that he could mount a stair rising from his dais and join his lady in their chamber without getting wet (Fig 37). When added to the end of a hall, always set at right angles to its axis, these two-storeyed houses or chambers were known to the contemporary builder as cross-chambers.

This brings us to the form of the manor house as established at the close of the thirteenth century, the barn-like hall having at its upper end, away from the hall-door, the small two-storeyed cross-chamber appearing as a wing to the hall. It is from this arrangement that the big house, as opposed to the farmhouse, develops. Meanwhile the 'cottages' of the medieval peasantry remained do-it-yourself hovels of poles and thatch.

In the days before banks, the lower storey of the cross-chamber was the treasury or 'wardrobe' of the lord of the manor house. The junction of the two structures made it possible for a doorway to be contrived at the back of the dais for entry to this apartment. And by the Tudor era the lord had taken a leaf out of the farmer's book and converted his erstwhile wardrobe into a privy parlour.

The visitor to the old manor house open today to the public soon becomes as familiar with its layout as its original builder (see Fig 38).

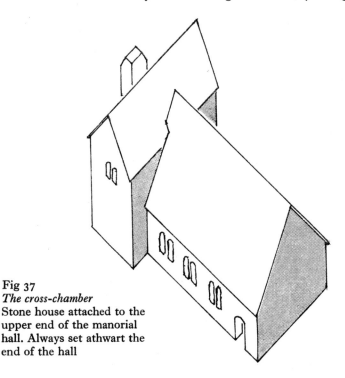

Fig 37
The cross-chamber
Stone house attached to the upper end of the manorial hall. Always set athwart the end of the hall

At first the hearth was probably central, with a louvred turret constructed among the rafters to carry away the smoke. Later, a cavernous fireplace under a wide arch would have been provided in the back wall of the hall, opposite the entrance façade. In late halls, the fireplace is sometimes set at the back of the dais, that stage raised above the 'marsh' of straw scavenged by dogs in the body of the hall. At the end of the dais next the entrance façade there is usually an extra-large window, sometimes a tall bay of many lights set between mullions and transoms of stone or wood.

At the lower or entrance end of the hall there stands the great

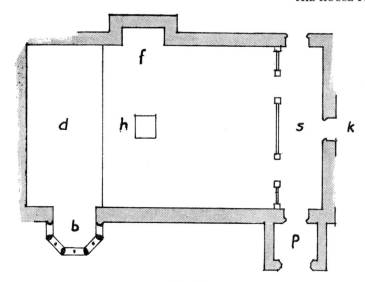

Fig 38
The medieval hall
Fundamental feature of the manor house: above the central hearth (h)
the dais (d) with its large window (b); at the lower end of the hall the
screens passage (s) entered from the entrance porch (p); by the Tudor
period the fire had been moved from the central hearth into a proper wall-
fireplace (f); the kitchen is at (k)

screen, spread across the apartment to obstruct draughts from the hall
doorway. Usually it has two doors through it indicating the position of
the long table which ran down the centre of the hall (see Fig 31).
Behind the screen is the passage known as 'the screens' leading by
another door to the kitchen with its offices, provided in an out-
building.

Towards the end of the medieval period a kitchen was built at the
lower end of the hall and reached from 'the screens' by a short passage,
on either side of which were a pantry for bread and a buttery for
drink. Halls thus equipped had in the rear wall of 'the screens' three
doors leading to the kitchen and its two offices (Fig 39). Sometimes
instead of the side doors there were just two hatches.

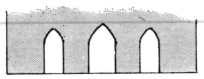

Fig 39
The hall doors
At the lower end of the hall one may often
find the kitchen doorway flanked by doors
leading into pantry and buttery

The great hall was lit by tall windows set along the entrance front; these, combined with the tall terminal features of bay window and tower porch, formed an impressive façade. The upper floor of the porch was often used to store muniments away from the damp.

The medieval period—the age of masonry—saw the building of many fine stone manor houses (Fig 40). But after the reduction in the mason strength which accompanied the decline in the fortunes of the great abbeys, manor-house builders began to turn to the very flourishing body of house-wrights who were now exhibiting their prowess by raising tall many-jettied town houses as well as rural farmhouses. Thus

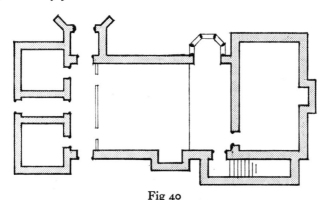

Fig 40
The Tudor manor house
Note the 'great parlour' behind the dais, the stair leading to the
'great chamber' over this, and at the lower end of the hall the
pantry and buttery flanking the passage leading to the kitchen

England is fortunate in still possessing many fine manor houses planned in the same way as the traditional stone buildings but framed up with timber screenwork set between heavy posts in the familiar fashion of the Tudors.

The cross-chamber developed from the twelfth-century King John's houses became in the hands of the carpenters a kind of standard unit with an upper floor jettied out at the gable ends. These units were built on to the broad single-storeyed hall in exactly the same fashion as could have been seen in the masonry prototypes.

Following the acceptance of the timber-framed manor house in those areas where the carpenters were dominant, diminutives of them began to appear—those delightful yeomen's houses which can still be found in scores scattered about villages and the countryside (Fig 41).

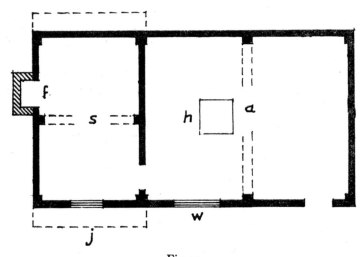

Fig 41
The yeoman's house
Timber-framed, it has its hall and parlour. Above the hearth (h) is the high timber arch (a), while across the parlour ceiling runs a heavy beam or summer supporting the joists of the chamber floor, the ends of which project as jetties (j) over the end wall (see Fig 11) to complete what is in fact a timber copy of the cross-chamber (see Fig 37). At (f) is the parlour fireplace; above it is another for the chamber

The chamber of such a house may have provided its only sleeping accommodation. But some houses had a small wing at the lower end of the hall containing the two important storerooms, pantry and buttery, and this was usually raised to match that at the upper end and give a second chamber. Thus we start to discover the beginnings of a wing balancing the original one, thus apparently introducing the symmetrical house-front (Fig 42).

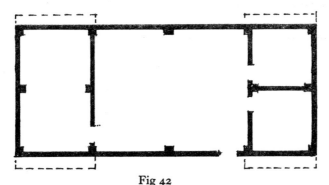

Fig 42
Double-ended house
Storerooms (see Fig 40) have been added at the lower end
of the hall and an upper storey raised over them to form a
second cross-chamber

Beside each cross-chamber rose a tall stack containing fireplaces for the parlour below and the chamber above, the latter with its tall roof carried by an arched truss, a miniature of that over the hall itself. The parlour fireplace had now become an architectural feature rivalling that in the hall; in hall-houses with a central hearth, the parlour fireplace was the principal feature of the house. With the flooring-over of the old open halls which was completed during the Elizabethan era, a stack had to be built at the back of the hall to take the new fireplace.

These yeomen's houses with their halls and cross-chambers were of course derived from the medieval manor house. By the end of the sixteenth century no more were being built. Their day was over; the house plan was developing not from the manor house but from the humble farmhouse with its kitchen and parlour.

The great step forward was the addition of a sleeping floor. This meant a chimney stack, and this started the chimney-building boom which so astonished William Harrison, possibly unaware of the reason for it. Hitherto, all chimneys had been built on to the side of a house, a situation introducing the complication of the chimney gutter. During the sixteenth century, however, the long farmhouse with the central passage which had existed since early medieval days began to provide itself with an internal fireplace arranged along the side of the passage

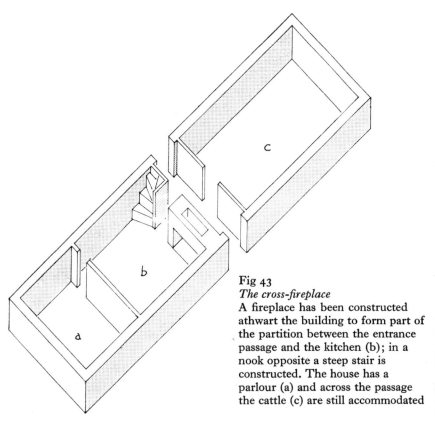

Fig 43
The cross-fireplace
A fireplace has been constructed athwart the building to form part of the partition between the entrance passage and the kitchen (b); in a nook opposite a steep stair is constructed. The house has a parlour (a) and across the passage the cattle (c) are still accommodated

next the living portion of the house (Fig 43). This had the effect of cutting away a number of floor joists above and this gap provided an excellent site for a proper stair fitted in next to the stack, a position it held for more than a century.

It was however at about this time that the cattle came to be evicted from the farmhouse, leaving the house part at last independent of them, to be seen as a pair of rooms, kitchen and parlour, each with its fireplace (Fig 44), the prototype of the farmhouse of the future.

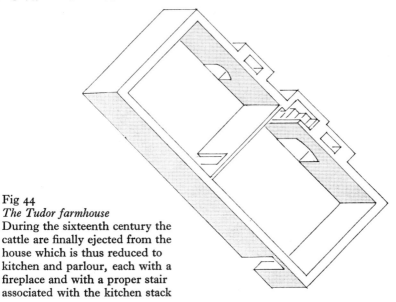

Fig 44
The Tudor farmhouse
During the sixteenth century the cattle are finally ejected from the house which is thus reduced to kitchen and parlour, each with a fireplace and with a proper stair associated with the kitchen stack

By the introduction of the internal fireplace into this two-part plan a standard arrangement was achieved which was to be adopted by the grantees of the monastic lands when building their new houses, and which continued throughout the next century to form the most common type of English farmhouse encountered today.

The plan was to erect a massive chimney stack having on either side of it a fireplace for the kitchen and for the parlour. It is these great stacks which appear everywhere brooding over the rural farmhouse and

rising above the roofs of the village street. On the entrance side of the
stack is formed an internal porch giving access to the two rooms while
on the opposite side is sited the timber stair winding round its mast-like
newel (Fig 45).

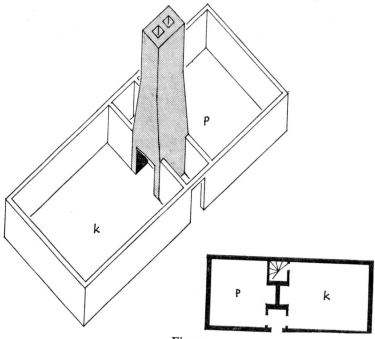

Fig 45
The central stack
The erection of a stack having kitchen and parlour fireplaces incorporated
within it provides the nucleus of the seventeenth-century standard farmhouse.
In the plan shown the rooms have been changed about to indicate that the plan
can be mirrored. On one side of the stack is the entrance porch and on the other
a spiral stair climbing up a mast (see also Fig 63)

Before the enclosures of the latter part of the eighteenth century
established the modern farm with the farmer living in a house
built on it, the farmer went each day to his strips in the common
fields but lived in a house set with others in a village or—as it is still

called in Australia—a township. Some of these settlements were openly planned, others huddled together as though for mutual shelter. Some were focused around a village green while others straggled along a street.

In the market towns, however, especially those defended by fortifications once so prominent, a system of close concentration was followed. Through the constricted areas, the narrow lanes threaded from gate to gate, passing the market place on their way. Since about the eleventh century, building plots had been established along these lanes, each having a frontage of some sixteen to twenty feet. Though each plot might be rebuilt or refronted time and time again, the rhythm of the frontage remained unbroken and overall harmony was maintained.

After the close of the sixteenth century, however, and the introduction of the long farmhouse, plots came to be joined together to accommodate these. This resulted in a noticeable change in the appearance of the frontage, for what had been a row of gable-ends now appeared as a series of roofs running parallel to the street. And in the centre of each long roof line rose one of the massive chimney stacks of the period, fixing the skyline of the street up to the present day.

The general rhythm of the street's fenestration was, however, maintained, changes being mainly in connection with the insertion of more fashionable windows. It is only in recent years that the rhythm of street frontages has been gravely damaged.

We have watched the upper end of the manor-house plan developing with the transformation of the old wardrobe of the cross-chamber into a privy parlour. During the fourteenth century this was being used as a dining room by the family seeking to escape the noise beyond the dais of 'poor men eating'. The move, however, had the effect of so lengthening the distance from the kitchen to the table that the food arrived chillier than ever. During the fifteenth century, therefore, they began to consider providing a special dining parlour somewhere nearer the lower end of the hall where the kitchen was situated. This winter parlour, as it was called, was first attached to the rear wall of the hall but eventually came to be sited in a wing at the lower end of the hall, balancing the great parlour itself. Thus we find a break in the long tradition of keeping the family away from the lower end of the house, and also an architectural innovation suggesting an imminent symmetry of layout expressed by a central block terminating in two wings, soon to be followed by the 'double-ended' yeomen's houses.

The introduction of a second parlour was a revolutionary step which was to affect the plans of the long farmhouses of the seventeenth century many of which added dining parlours to the lower ends of their kitchens (Fig 46). This had the interesting result of removing the entrance doorway from its central position beneath the great stack and sending it back to its traditional situation at the lower end of the living room (see Fig 46). The old entrance porch became an intercommunicating lobby. The new parlour had to be provided with its own chimney stack.

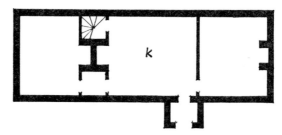

Fig 46
Two-parlour farmhouse
Also typical of the seventeenth century and forming
the principal type of building lining the village street.
A lower or dining parlour has been added with its own
fireplace. The entrance doorway has been restored to
its traditional position at the lower end of the living
room: it is usually covered with a porch (see Fig 64)

It will be noted that after the introduction of the internal stack at the end of the sixteenth century all chimney stacks come to be absorbed within the outer walls of the house instead of projecting as hitherto. From the seventeenth century onwards we find the fireplace flanked by two recesses an almost universal arrangement.

It is difficult to imagine nowadays the appearance of this country after the suppression of the great abbeys in 1539. The countryside must have presented an extraordinary spectacle with scores of huge monastic complexes—far bigger than the largest palace and vying even with great castles in extent—lying deserted except for gangs of looters and demolition squads.

The disposal of these huge buildings and their materials had actually brought about the rise of a new profession—that of surveyor. From the surveying of existing buildings to the designing of new ones was not a very long step, especially as the surveyors had perforce to learn how to draw plans. Thus out of the company of surveyors employed by the monastic grantees there were some who rose to be architects.

The history of architecture generally follows fairly smoothly along foreseeable lines. But in the history of the English great house continuity was broken when the professional architect born of the Renaissance movement came upon the scene. His appearance coincided with the visible destruction of the existing, medieval, world—the new architects could hardly pretend any enthusiasm for perpetuating an art which they could see collapsing in ruin about them.

For all that, however, the first houses raised by the Elizabethans were basically medieval, in that the old hall, nucleus of the great house from beyond memory, was retained as indispensable to dignity. Nevertheless, the soaring apartment of the medieval noble could not possibly have been incorporated into the lines of a Renaissance *palazzo*. Thus, while accepted on plan, the Elizabethan great hall lost most of its third dimension and was brought down to storey height so that the chamber floor could pass unbroken across it. It was this continuous upper floor which was probably the most important Elizabethan contribution to the English house plan, to be echoed throughout all, even the humblest, English homes.

At this time we find a great increase in the number of separate rooms for guests. The turning of roof spaces into bedchambers was copied enthusiastically by the farmers. The Elizabethan determination to increase accommodation resulted in the expansion of the cross-chamber

F

into a long wing. During this transformation the great parlour remained but the great chamber was moved to above the lowered hall where it became known as the *salon*.

Medieval planning had been dictated by convenience only. But under the influence of the Renaissance the English architect now had to consider planning for presentation—and symmetrical presentation at that! This meant that the great hall had to be balanced beyond its porch by another block of apartments (see Fig 47). Hereabouts might be a spacious hall around which a fine staircase might rise towards the *salon*. The winter parlour could be sited here, close to kitchens sited at the rear of the nearby wing.

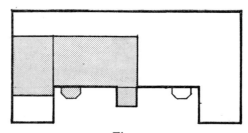

Fig 47
The Elizabethan mansion
Developed as indicated by taking the medieval manor house and duplicating it beyond the entrance porch so as to provide a symmetrical Renaissance façade

The new houses of the Elizabethan magnates seem so alike as almost to appear as though they were planned by the same architect. Completely novel in plan and presentation, they all have the central block with its porch forming a focal feature, the whole flanked by its long wings of lodgings. Sometimes these were extended forward by garden walls to enclose a forecourt entered by an imposing gateway facing the tall house-porch.

We can detect little affinity, beyond the continuous upper floor, between the great house of the Elizabethan magnate and the contemporary farmhouse. The former had chimney stacks arranged about it in medieval fashion but with possibly a single internal stack to accommodate the hall fireplace. The great stack of the farmhouse had been introduced as a measure of planning economy.

This central stack, however, was found to have two grave disadvantages. It formed a massive obstruction to the circulation within the house and prevented the replacement of the obsolete spiral stair by one of the new 'dog-legs' of Commonwealth days. Another inconvenient feature—to be experienced to this day—was that the fireplaces of both rooms were set next to the entrance doors to the rooms so that no one could sit in comfort in front of the fire without being plagued by draughts from these, and from the front door itself if the house should be of the single-parlour type.

Thus with the ending of the seventeenth century the great stacks, which had served their owners so well for more than a hundred years and formed the skyline to many a town street, were abandoned to history and replaced by the arrangement, which has remained ever since, of setting the chimneys on either side of the house, bestowing upon it that special 'rabbit's-ears' silhouette of the eighteenth and nineteenth centuries which contrasts so strongly with the single-stack sturdiness of the seventeenth-century house.

With the vastly more elaborate house plans of the Elizabethan era the need for internal partitioning became acute, and the joiners were set to work to design these. The old type of screen with its vertical muntins was modified by introducing horizontal rails so as to form square panels. The seventeenth century became the age of panelling.

The removal of the central stack which had hitherto provided a division between the two main rooms of the farmhouse necessitated a fresh look also at partitioning arrangements for the humbler type of building. Panelling begins to appear in these also, though in many cases the old studded screens had to suffice. It should be remembered that seventeenth-century partitioning, while employed in separating rooms, did not concern itself with what we call circulation, which means access to any room without passing through another. It is this complete lack of circulation which makes it so difficult to convert houses of this period to modern requirements. Corridors did not come in until the next century when the double-span plan and the central staircase changed the situation in the centre of the house.

During the seventeenth century we find standing between the farmhouse and the mansion a new type of house, what we might call the house of the squire. Such a house is in reality the manor house transformed unrecognisably into a small Renaissance villa.

The mansions of the Elizabethans had been roofed in single spans, a second span being added behind that accommodating the great hall and the *salon*, the intervening valley being efficiently waterproofed by the plumbers. The double gables at either end of this central block (see Fig 48a) were completely masked by the long wings which had developed from the cross-chambers of medieval days.

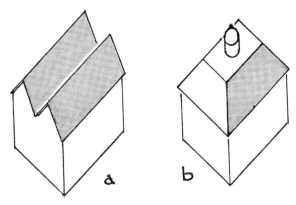

Fig 48
The Renaissance roof
Medieval roofs were all single-span, spanning from one wall to that opposite. Setting two such roofs side by side (a) led to the formation of a deep 'valley' which trapped snow and led damp into the building. Hence the introduction of the double-span roof (b) a single wide-span roof embracing both the original structures. To avoid making this of a monstrous size it was often 'hipped' all round (see Fig 24), a lead-covered flat roof being set above the middle of the house

The rectangular house of the squire, however, lacking the convenient wings, had to adopt another system of roofing, the double-span, which covered both the front and back portions of the house with a single tall roof, in this case hipped round the ends. In order to avoid having to complete this as a pyramid, however, it was truncated and a lead-covered flat roof thrown over the centre of the house (Fig 48b). This completed the Englishman's version of a Renaissance villa—though of course the roof of the original would have been either flat or of a far lower pitch than could have been permitted by the English climate.

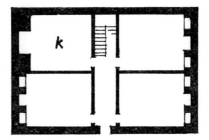

Fig 49
The square house
The two portions of a double-span house joined together became replanned as two pairs of rooms, 'front and back', separated by a staircase hall

In its simplest form, the squire's house plan comprised a central staircase hall with two rooms on either side, their fireplaces represented by four chimney stacks set on the flanks of the house (Fig 49). From this simple mid-seventeenth-century layout two important types of plan developed. The deep double-span arrangement which had at last taken the place of the long-established medieval system was having the effect of setting rooms one behind the other instead of end to end. This had long been the custom in the town house set on its narrow frontage with its gable-end to the street. The plan of the fifteenth- and sixteenth-century town house had been a shop with a storeroom behind it, hall and parlour on the floor above, and bedchambers above these.

By taking the plan of the squire's house and removing one of the pairs of parlours flanking the central stair, this and the two remaining parlours could be set on a narrow urban plot as a 'single-fronted' house. It was indeed this unit, repeated many times, which provided the basis for the long terraces of houses built by speculators after the end

of the Civil War and employed in developing the suburbs of London
(Fig 50).

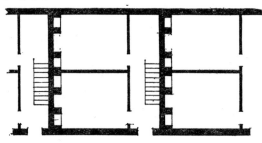

Fig 50
The terrace house
The unit formed by the
'front and back' with its
staircase hall became
assembled into terraces of
small houses set along
urban streets

It was during the eighteenth century that at long last we find true
cottages appearing as an item in English architecture. This was due to
he enterprise of the Georgian farmer who took sufficient pride in his
estate to include the proper housing of his farm-people amongst his
operations, employing builders whom the labourer wanting a decent
home would have been quite unable to pay.

It was at this time that the discovery was made that the building unit
of 'front and back and pair of stairs' could be economically combined
with a party wall between them to form a pair of cottages. This is the
origin of that now universal house-type, the semi-detached (Fig 51).

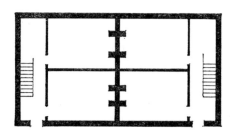

Fig 51
The semi-detached
Pairs of the units referred to in
Fig 50 provided cottages for
farm-labourers of the eighteenth
and nineteenth centuries and are
perpetuated in the semi-
detached pairs seen in the
housing estates of the present
day

Despite the popularity of the urban terrace, however, the symmetri-
cally fronted house of the rural squire had set a fashion which could not
be ignored. With parlours on either side of the front door it formed
what was known as a double-fronted house, whereas the terrace house

was only single-fronted. As recently as the early years of this century the social difference between the two types was understood by suburban householders.

At the end of the well-organised eighteenth century every township had its company of small tradesmen—tailor, breeches maker, bootmaker, glover—who worked at home, these in addition to the baker, carpenter, smith, saddler and wheelwright, who had workshops attached to their homes. The houses of the small tradesman of the day are now easily recognisable, each being a single-span copy of the squire's house with a parlour on each side of the front door leading into a narrow staircase hall. Above are three bedroom windows; the roof ends in gables each with its little chimney. Renaissance in miniature, they contrast unmistakably with the long farmhouse of the seventeenth century with its central stack (Fig 52).

Fig 52
Artisan's house
Tradesmen who could afford to engage a builder erected double-fronted cottages each completely detached and with the entrance doorway set in the centre of the house front. Single-span only, each had a kitchen and parlour in the old fashion

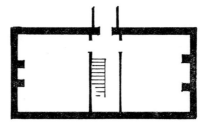

It was probably not until the latter part of the eighteenth century that the really poor farm-labourer was able to build for himself something resembling what we would call today a cottage. When the Enclosure Acts began to take effect on the farming community, many old buildings—small farmhouses and their buildings—became derelict. Salvaged materials from these could be used to build humble homes for victims of the Agricultural Revolution. Enough whole bricks could be salvaged from ruins to build a chimney stack, while broken 'bats' could be used to 'nog' rough panels of a house-frame knocked together from second-hand timbers. In the field-stone regions it would have been even easier to raise a hovel with a chimney stack forming part of a gable-end. A doorway, a window for a little light when this was closed, and a boarded loft reached by a ladder would complete the cottage (Figs 53 and 54).

Fig 53
The timber-framed 'cot'
During the eighteenth century a man without funds could accumulate enough second-hand materials to build, with his friends' help, a very small cottage. The main problem would be to find mortar for the chimney stack

Fig 54
The field-stone hovel
Stone gathered from the fields could be set in clay and plastered with the same material

During this period when the farming plan of England was being completely rearranged, many of the old long houses which had served the country so well were allowed to stand. Some of them were modernised by having a new house built across the parlour end (Fig 55) retaining the old farmhouse kitchen with its great fireplace for cooking. The old part of the house then became what the Americans—whose houses were at this period following much the same development—call the 'ell'. These L-shaped houses are frequently met with in England.

But the more common fate of the old long house was for it to be divided into what today we call a row of cottages (Fig 56). It is amusing to hear people describing how they are ennobling their row of cottages to form a house, not realising that what they are really doing is restoring it to its former glory.

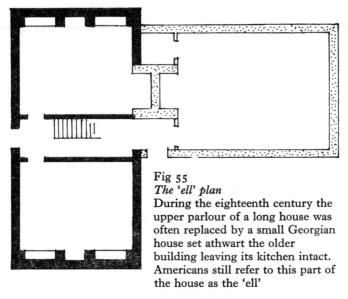

Fig 55
The 'ell' plan
During the eighteenth century the
upper parlour of a long house was
often replaced by a small Georgian
house set athwart the older
building leaving its kitchen intact.
Americans still refer to this part of
the house as the 'ell'

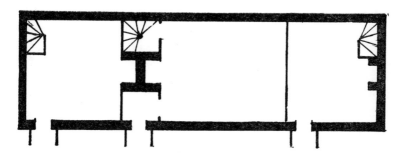

Fig 56
The 'row of cottages'
With many small farmers ruined by the Enclosure Acts of the late
eighteenth and early nineteenth centuries their houses were converted
into rows of cottages by the farmers who bought them out

The terrace plan flourished. From beginnings in Bloomsbury it expanded into the palatial terraces of Bayswater and Belgravia. Taken up by speculative builders all over the country it created the glorious terraces of Georgian Bath, and on a much reduced scale provided homes for wage-earners in country towns.

Where land was less valuable, semi-detached pairs could be set on plots which made possible the provision of back gardens wider than those which extended behind a terrace, while the old economy of saving a wall was maintained. One of the odd features of early twentieth-century 'housing schemes' was that if the plots did not work out in pairs it was considered quite satisfactory to erect half a pair!

In the inner suburbs, terraces; in the outer, semi-detached. In this way the towns were expanding their limits with types of houses new to architecture.

Provision for hospitality is not a function of the normal house plan but may be important in the larger house. The banqueting hall of the Middle Ages, and even its pale successor in the Elizabethan mansion, had vanished from the scene, but the owners of houses above a certain class still needed to give an occasional party. The squire's house had its parlours, but these were squarish and soon appeared crowded. The tall terrace house of the late eighteenth and early nineteenth centuries often had wide folding doors introduced between front and back parlours so as create a 'drawing room'— reversing its original purpose of 'withdrawing room' and making it a kind of privately owned assembly room. A feature introduced during the Regency was the bowed end, like a flattish apse, with large windows in it.

During the Early-Victorian period, the days of Pickwick and gargantuan meals, the dining room became the principal room of the house. Frequently it was made to project as a wing ending in a three-sided bay. Often it adjoined the front door of the house, as though advertising its social status (Fig 57).

This was perhaps the first indication of future degeneracy in the house plan, for the dining-room bay was added merely as an excrescence and played no part in the elevational design. It had the effect of ruining the entrance doorway and making it impossible to provide a good porch. This lop-sided plan with the cramped entrance persisted for a century; even between the two world wars it was still bedevilling suburban houses.

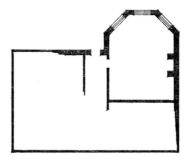

Fig 57
The dining-room bay
During the Early-Victorian period the fashion for giving dinner parties led to the enlargement of the dining parlour, often by adding a projecting end to it flanking the front entrance

The dining-room bay was echoed in the little turnpike toll-houses of the period, each of which had a similar bay with a doorway facing the gate and windows looking up and down the road. With the bay window reintroduced in its new clumsiness into ordinary domestic architecture it begins to appear everywhere in Victorian houses, often only one storey high, projecting from the principal living rooms.

The development of that superior hovel, the bungalow, will be examined later. Its plan is based upon entirely different factors from those which inspired the English house plan and nowadays often achieves what is known as the open plan, comprising a central area from which all other rooms are entered.

One should not close this brief discussion of the English house plan without reminding the reader that all plans are but traces upon the ground, or on paper, and must always be scanned with three-dimensional vision, raising every wall to its ceiling and covering the whole with a tall roof in English fashion.

CHAPTER THREE

THE NATURE OF ARCHITECTURE

IN THE last chapter we examined the changing requirements of the English home-builder as he passed on his way along the centuries, while in the previous one we discussed the various methods available to him towards satisfying these requirements. The combination of these two elements, the requirement and the means, produces architecture. This is not to say, however, that buildings of outstanding beauty will result—though as a matter of fact there are few houses, not even excepting some of those more recently built, which do not carry something of that atmosphere which always accompanies the home of a family.

The house plan, and the structure founded upon it, create a building. It is this public display of a building constructed for some purpose not necessarily known to us, and by methods of which we may have no knowledge, that constitutes what we mean by architecture.

The visual appeal of much architecture may be entirely fortuitous, owing nothing to the skill of the designer. Nowadays, for instance, much of the attraction of, say, a medieval manor house may be largely attributable to a sentimental regard for a building illustrating an era in the social history of our forebears, and owing nothing to architectural appreciation.

During the last four to five centuries our most important buildings have been designed by professional architects, who estimate what they hope to be the external effect of the completed building when preparing what is known as its elevations. In early days the elevations just 'happened'—doors and windows, porches and chimney stacks, were accepted as mere vertical projections of items set out on the plan of the accommodation. Each feature followed the aesthetic form accepted at the period, but the grouping was fortuitous and not specially designed.

The manor house, the only considerable domestic building of the Middle Ages, consisted of a great hall having a row of tall windows set along it, that at the 'upper' end being either larger than the others or a projecting bay window. At the 'lower' end of the hall was a projecting porch. Next to the hall bay one would find the tall wing containing the great chamber with its special window forming a feature of the upper storey beneath the gable (Fig 58). In later days this might be a pro-

Fig 58
The medieval manor house
For its plan see Fig 40; the kitchen and offices are not however shown here

Fig 59
The Tudor manor house
This is shown in its timber-framed form

jecting oriel carried on ornamental brackets, while below it the elevation might have launched out into a good window lighting the great parlour. At first, the high roof of the hall would have been capped with a turret to vent the smoke but later we should see the top of a tall chimney stack appearing behind the ridge. The styles of doorways and windows would change, their tops becoming less acute as the fifteenth century approached. The tracery of the hall windows would expand into flowing forms and die away again into sterner panelling.

In the fifteenth century, with the mason giving place to the house-wright, we see the whole appearance of the manor house undergoing a dramatic change as sturdy walling gives place to light timbered screens pierced with slender-mullioned windows instead of the heavy stone tracery. The cross-chamber at the upper end of the hall—and perhaps another at the lower end—are jettied out over the lower storey. The cross-chamber—raised perhaps to include a third storey—becomes the tall town house on its single narrow plot. A double-plot might accommodate a hall-house with a central hearth.

Then with fireplaces coming into use everywhere during the second half of the sixteenth century the hall soon disappears and we find long houses with the close timbering of the period, two-storeyed throughout, the whole of the upper floor jettied out over the street (Fig 60). It was

Fig 60
The fully jettied house
Here the yeoman's house plan (Fig 41) has been absorbed into a single structure having a complete upper storey above a low kitchen instead of a lofty hall; the whole of the upper floor has been jettied out over the lower

this type of house which formed the standard design of the period and which eventually led to the seventeenth-century long house with its central stack piercing the ridge of the roof. But until this arrived, the kitchen stack was built against the back of the house, with probably another for the parlour alongside. (See Fig 44).

It was the fate of many jetties to lose their projection with the coming of bricks which were used to build up under them to carry the sills of the upper storey (see Fig 61). Examination of the ceiling of a ground-floor room in an old house which has been widened in this fashion will usually disclose the notches in the joists where the head of the vanished timber wall was once housed.

Fig 61
Under-building the jetty
In this house the front wall of the parlour has been built out on brick or stone to the limit of the jetty over; many old jetties have disappeared in the course of this operation

It has always been an article of faith with good architects that the higher, and therefore the more visibly, a building should rise, the more care should be given to its architectural presentation. This attitude was the source of the magnificent church towers of the fifteenth century. And when these were being built no more, their place on the Elizabethan skyline was taken by a forest of chimneys, their great stacks crowned by flues presented as miniature pillars like those of a church, each with its base, cap, and a shaft which was sometimes worked as a spiral. It is these chimney tops which formed the architectural climax to many a comparatively humble farmhouse of Elizabethan days.

The provision of wall-fireplaces with their flues removed any obstacle to having upper floors. The first or chamber floor was soon followed by the attic storey, no mere loft but accommodation which at the time would have been considered reasonably comfortable. To light the rooms an array of side gables appears along the building, each with its gable window. It is this many-gabled effect which is so characteristic of Elizabethan architecture, particularly attractive as distributed throughout the Cotswolds (Fig 62).

Elizabethan windows lacked the beauty of the Gothic forms, but this became inevitable when masonry walling gave place to timber frames into the rectangular panels which of the windows had to be fitted (this was one of the factors which transformed the flowing lines of the Decorated period into the panelling of the Perpendicular. Thus rectangular windows became the rule, though some of these were quite extensive in area and were divided up by systems of mullions and transoms into a multitude of lights. Elizabethan architects made the most of fenestration, lively as ever with a scintillating pattern of leaded lights.

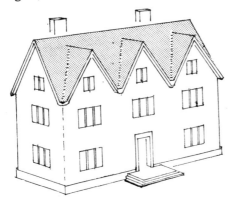

Fig 62
Many-gabled house
In order to light the attic of the Elizabethan house its front was gabled to take windows

It was at the middle of the sixteenth century that the English carpenter came into his own as a builder not only of houses but of palaces such as that of Nonsuch, in the Surrey fringe of London, with its elaborate timberwork lively to a degree never before experienced in architecture. This was a palace of Henry VIII, but his daughter Elizabeth began to appreciate that this prodigal squandering of the country's forests could not be allowed to continue and began to demand a more scientific approach to timber construction which would eliminate the close-studded frame. So at the time of Shakespeare's plays we find the Jacobean style beginning to take shape, panelled frames with here and there a raking brace (see Fig 13). Thus the Tudor heyday of the English carpenter proved to be but an Indian summer, with bricks just over the horizon to take over the task of house construction.

The long houses of the seventeenth century remain the most easily recognisable style of farmhouse architecture to be found in village and countryside, the central stack being the distinguishing feature. The

Cotswold houses are, for the most part, of this period and show central and gable stacks, have side gables to their attics, and the typical stone-mullioned windows of Elizabethan and Jacobean days.

The single-parlour house (Fig 63) presents the basic type of elevation,

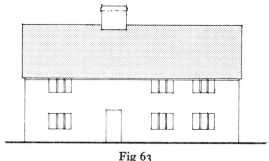

Fig 63
Seventeenth-century farmhouse
See Fig 45 for plan

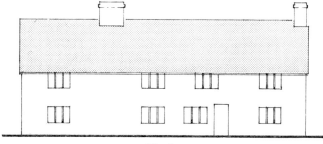

Fig 64
Two-parlour farmhouse
See Fig 46 for plan

but the longer house with the winter parlour at the lower end of the kitchen exists beside it; this type has the entrance doorway away from the stack (Figs 64 and 65). It is this type which, its entrance lacking the inner lobby of the single-parlour house, often throws out an external one. It is inside these doorways that one may find well-joinered screens, often simply moulded. High-backed settles are part of the furniture of

G

houses of this period, as well as permanent benches forming part of the screens. The trestle table and the gate-leg table are among the other items of furniture associated with the long houses.

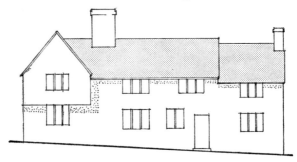

Fig 65
The sloping street
Timber-framed houses could be constructed room by room. Thus it was an easy matter to set even the long double-parlour house on a sloping site. Here the upper part of the house has been constructed as a cross-chamber (see Fig 37)

These houses cannot be mistaken for those of the two centuries following, as the central stack disappears and the two lateral stacks on the gables completely change the appearance of the farmhouse and draw attention to the symmetrical elevation with its central doorway below.

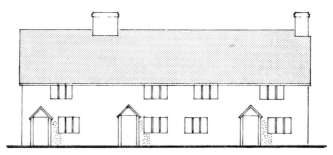

Fig 66
The 'row of cottages'
See also Fig 56

The squire's house of the Stuart period is seen as a square block, basically Renaissance but with the tall English roof giving it its own distinction. Its windows are usually a derivation of the Elizabethan but with the horizontal transom raised above the centre line to give it a cruciform shape. (see Fig 84b). The Elizabethan window usually had its transom lowered so that the lower light could be opened as a casement; later casements may have been made more strongly so that opening lights could be taller.

The tall Stuart window, designed to conform with the window proportion required by Renaissance architecture, does not appear in the farmhouse which remains faithful to a two- or three-light mullioned window of low proportions, a type of window which never died out except for the replacement of iron casements with joinered ones.

Every medieval house had been entered by what one might call the front door, which was the hall door of the manor house or just the kitchen door of the farmhouse. Thus every building, large and small, had what might be called its entrance front, the elevation which it presented towards the returning owner or his visitor. It should appear as welcoming and was seldom repellent. Its most important architectural feature would probably have been the entrance porch, an appendage which the climate rendered essential for all houses. Should the approaching visitor glance about him at the rest of the façade—perhaps in order to try to assess the wealth of its owner—he might not, until the Tudor period, observe any indication that it had been designed for this purpose.

It was at the Tudor period that the development of the hall bay in magnificent style, and the introduction of a tower-porch, worthy of a church, balancing this, began to show a tendency towards the presentation of a façade, a device unknown to the Gothic architect who had just accepted buildings as they came. Elevational treatments were still restricted to individual features and there was no attempt to group them as an entity. The architectural elevation had yet to come.

It did so entirely under the aegis of the Italian Renaissance, with its visible ordinance or system of rules, its discoverable rules of composition which could guide as well as control the design of a house-front.

The Renaissance style was essentially a rectangular one. Although for the time being English architects had to accept the English snow-shedding roof pitch, the wall-faces below were rectangular, and the windows in them the same (Fig 67). The gable had to go, to be replaced by hipped ends.

Fig 67
The small Renaissance house
See Fig 49 for plan

The great Elizabethan mansions had made much play with repetitions of tall bay windows, which with the tall chimney stacks emphasised that element of verticality so important in a monumental façade. But the requirements of the Renaissance insisted that all such excrescences were planed away, though verticality was maintained to some extent by a few tall chimney stacks set about the tall roofs to maintain the spirit of winter Englishry.

Symmetry in presentation was fundamental to the Renaissance elevational system. The front door was in the centre of the façade. It took some time to persuade the English house-builder that in the interests of the sunnier Italian architecture he must abandon his welcoming porch and exchange it for a door-case of Classical detail with flanking pilasters, a cornice over, and possibly a pediment (Fig 68).

The Classical cornice was an essential feature of the Renaissance building (see Fig 79). But it was not so easy to introduce this into the spreading eaves of a tall English roof, especially if it was thatched as many quite large houses still were. In dealing with thatch, the English device was to compromise by striking a wide plaster cove under the eaves of the thatch as a kind of gesture towards a cornice, but as the use of tiling made the situation more manageable the complete cornice with its elaborate mouldings and array of little brackets called modillions were all provided to complete the Renaissance elevation. A very plain form of the medieval parapet with its gutter behind it was also introduced to facilitate the provision of the all-important cornice. During the eighteenth century pediments were displayed on many house-fronts, over the entrance doorway and often as a central feature breaking the main cornice above this.

Fig 68
The pediment
One of the principal features of
Renaissance architecture, often
set in the centre of the façade
and above windows and entrance
doorways

The real glory of the squire's house—one capable of being enjoyed at a distance—was its fenestration. After the cruciform windows of the early Stuart era with their old-fashioned leaded casements came the tall sash windows of the age of Wren. At first the glazing bars were sturdy and the panes almost square, but during the eighteenth century the bars became more slender and the proportion of width to height of the panes about two to three. As the Regency period approached the bars became very slender and the panes more elongated.

The loss of the porch was probably resented by the house-owner of the seventeenth century, its place being taken without much delay by a great door-hood, a feature exclusive to England and doubtless demanded by an irate squire after having to stand about in the rain trying to unearth his door-key. These heavy hoods of the late seventeenth century were carried upon massive brackets carved in the curly style of the Continental Baroque, a peculiarly English manifestation of this style of ornament—provided, aptly enough, to keep off the rain.

Towards the end of the century the porch proper was revived in a form again very English yet far removed from the cavernous entries of medieval days, the door-hood being projected from the house wall and carried at its outer angles by a pair of Classical columns. Such porches were a common feature of Regency houses and during their Gothic phase the Classical columns became copies of the clustered pillars of medieval days.

The charming style which replaced the rather more solid Georgian relied for much of its appeal upon the use of walling rendered and made to gleam with white paint. Regency fronts themselves were quite simple, but their plain walling provides a splendid canvas for a display of fenestration. There were many different types of windows, all with tall panes divided by slender glazing bars. Very popular was the Venetian window (Fig 85a) which had a tall centre portion covered with an arch and flanked by a pair of narrower windows covered with flat lintels. This is often the terminal window of the assembly room; it is always employed on its own so as to be spared competition.

A simpler form of the Venetian window, which one might call the triptych, had no arch and consisted of an ordinary Georgian window flanked by two others half the width (see Fig 85b). This type became very commonly used in country houses as well as in those being built in the suburbs of country towns. Triptych windows are usually set in vertical lines, one above the other, not in horizontal tiers as were the Georgian windows.

A special type of window appears above the door of the terrace house to light its overlong staircase hall. This is called today a fanlight as it later filled in the arched top of the doorway with a fan or spider's web of strips of lead, forming another peculiarly English feature of the Renaissance.

Perhaps the most striking of the early nineteenth-century windows is the very tall window lighting the staircase hall (see Fig 85c) often set above the stair itself and with a Gothic pattern of glazing bars clearly intended to be principal feature of the circulation within the house.

The bay window, once the special attribute of the nobleman in his great hall, became very popular on a much reduced scale as a feature of the urban Georgian house where it provided residents with an all-round view of the world outside. Such windows became fine pieces of joinery, usually with their own cornice treatments, and added considerably to the architectural interest of the house-front. Diminutive copies of the bay window were added in hundreds to the little houses in the streets of the eighteenth and nineteenth centuries. The pleasant little curved 'bow' window of the Regency introduced into these scenes the first 'modern' shop front.

Georgian was the national style of the England of the third quarter of the eighteenth century, immediately prior to the beginnings of the Industrial Revolution with its mills and factories. This was also the period of the beginning of the romantic novel as a literary form, and the historical novel of 'Gothic' style which revived an interest in the days of chivalry. Immersed in such relaxations, the leisured classes of England were beginning to discover a revulsion against the staidness of the square Georgian houses and a restored respect for the native traditions of England as illustrated by the remains of ruined abbeys and other relics of the medieval era. The result of this introspection was an attempt to revive the Gothic style of architecture.

It was a gallant effort, but ill-advised. There were no longer any masons capable of raising the stone buildings of the Middle Ages—nor, indeed, could anyone have afforded the current cost of such ventures. But it was discovered that Gothic detail—pointed arches, clustered pillars, mouldings, carved foliage even—could be introduced into the plain Georgian buildings by simply forming them in common brick and covering them with moulded plaster. And it was a simple matter to shape the glazing bars of windows into Gothic forms, thus transforming the building quickly from Renaissance to Gothic. In this simple fashion the Gothic of the Regency was introduced into hundreds of buildings of all descriptions throughout the country. It was a charming style, but one of ornament rather than sound architecture, and the fashion, like the materials in which it was presented, proved all too ephemeral.

It is tragic that a fashion so charmingly conceived by patriotism out
of frivolity should have so misled the public as to have been taken
seriously. Architecture is made of sterner stuff; structure and materials
are the only basis for its forms. And at the beginning of the last century
we find large country houses having plaster Gothic interiors cased in a
skin of hard-faced pseudo-Elizabethan masonry—a revival not of
treasured 'Gothick' fantasies but only recalling the opulent pride of the
wool magnate—the abode not of art and learning but of commerce.
The Gothic Revival of Victorian days is found to have little about it of
the Gothick whims of the Regency. We must surely owe a debt of
gratitude to the fairy-tale architects of the Regency who created those
enchanting dolls' houses with their pointed arches and leaded lattices
dotted about in town lanes and round the coves of the seaside.

But even such a minor revolution was bound to start a counter one,
and the danger was that the retort might be of a censorious nature and
result in an architecture even more severe than before. Indeed it came
soon enough, probably under the aegis of the more studious aesthetes
of the Regency world of fashion. The Grand Tour had been extended
eastwards into Greece where in Athens architectural purists now found
themselves able to study the origins of that Classical architecture a
modified ordinance of which they had been reproducing in its Renaissance guise. Unfortunately the explorers went too far back in antiquity
and introduced a fashion for the grim old Doric of the Parthenon with
its unattractively sturdy columns and crude capitals (Fig 69). But that

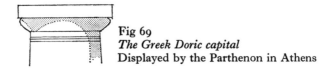

Fig 69
The Greek Doric capital
Displayed by the Parthenon in Athens

the latest architectural innovation was readily accepted is evidenced by
the massive Doric porches of squires' houses as well as public buildings
such as the inns and assembly rooms of the coaching era.

Both these Regency styles, the Gothic and the Greek, signalled an important phase in the history of English architecture—the sight of the end of the road. Revolutions are not the same as natural development, and this is essential to architecture. True historical development had in fact ended with the Georgian—revivals of past styles indicated not progress but decay. And while the grotesque conflict between the Classicists and the Gothicists—the latter quick to react to the Doric challenge—continued, no attempt could be made to check the decline and set English architecture on its feet again. It was at this period that England was setting the fashion for culture in Western Europe; thus while the Gothic Revival, being essentially English, had no effect upon the Continent, the Greek Revival was speedily followed and its influence extended from Scandinavia to Spain, this wrecking the architectural development of the Continent as well as that of England.

In England the Doric porch was the principal legacy of the Classicists. The Gothic in its Victorian form, however, may be seen everywhere, its hard-faced lines, generally mechanical Elizabethan cut in unsuitable stone, appearing most inappropriately in small and completely un-Gothic villas. So persistent was the fashion for Gothic that one finds everywhere hideous manifestations of Corinthianesque caps set beside door and window openings of repulsive *fin-de-siècle* villas in contemporary suburban development.

As the middle of the century approached, however, a third influence began to appear in the architectural world. The Gothic Revival was spreading itself around churches old and new, while the towering factories of the industrial towns made good use of the mighty Doric. But neither style, it was realised, could really be regarded as suitable for ordinary domestic architecture.

There were, however, a number of level-headed architects who could appreciate that the current revivals—'Romanesque' had now joined in—could only result in a complete collapse of orderly elevational presentation. They decided to cast back to the point where the history of architectural development had petered out, with the intention of starting again from there. By the beginning of the nineteenth century, most architects were studying the history of their craft, and there was

little difficulty in discovering that the last true historical style had been
the Italian Renaissance which in its modified Georgian form had
succeeded in establishing itself in England during the eighteenth
century.

From this point they cast back towards sources. But with more
restraint than the over-enthusiastic Classicists they decided to descend
from their mules at Rome, then a semi-ruinous village-city, Mecca of
the tourist, amongst the ancient relics of which they could admire the
decaying palaces of the Renaissance. Thus, approaching the second
half of the century, the English architect could spread himself with
confidence in the presentation of public buildings in irreproachable
Renaissance style.

But even this comparatively restrained style of architecture, like its
rival the Gothic and the Greek, was still quite unsuitable for use upon
the smaller house. For this purpose, the touring architects had to
explore Florence and the northern lakes to sketch the more light-
hearted Renaissance of the country villa.

The sketches they brought back were an instant success. As one
travels about England, especially in the Victorian suburbs, one cannot
fail to detect these Italian villas, the first indication in English architecture of the obsessive belief that by importing the architecture of a
sunnier land one would bring the sun with it. A feature of these
Italianesque villas of the mid-nineteenth century is the tall tower
(Fig 70)—possibly a descendant of the campanile of Florence
Cathedral—which nearly always appears attached to each. These
expensive towers can have served no useful purpose, even though the
little room at the summit approached by a steep stair might have a
view of sorts. But it seems clear that the campanile was the 1840 status
symbol, even quite small houses having a little tower attached to them.

The farmhouses pursued their course through the byways of
Victorian architecture, showing few signs of the turmoil raging over
their slate roofs. Boringly plain, they remained symmetrical in presentation between their ear-like chimney stacks. The introduction of gas-
lighting forced them to have higher ceilings to avoid asphyxiation—you

can still see the plaster 'rose' on which the gasolier once depended and which has retained the name even though it is now represented by a round block of wood—and this had the effect of extending the height of most buildings of the mid-nineteenth century. Large families, with more children surviving than in earlier days, suggested a second chamber floor as well as an attic lit by dormers. Height becomes a noticeable element of the Victorian farmhouse. At the rear of the building the old catslide may still sweep down over the outshot and bring this up a storey higher to increase the accommodation still further.

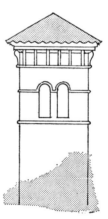

Fig 70
The campanile
A Florentine feature often attached
to Italianesque villas of about 1840

In high rooms, the sash window usually replaced the standard casement type with mullions. Glazing bars were generally retained, but by the middle of the century they were often omitted and the sashes filled with plain sheets of rolled glass which added to the dreariness of the farmhouse elevation.

But even in the humblest Early-Victorian house the Renaissance appears in one small detail. A feature of the massive overhanging cornice of the palace was the series of curved modillion brackets supporting its upper part. This device was copied by the Early-Victorian builders in humble form by providing wide eaves with a boarded 'soffit' and supporting this by an array of simple shaped brackets cut out of pine boards (see Fig 71). Above this curious cornice a roof of blue Welsh slates generally ended in low-pitched gables but was sometimes hipped all round.

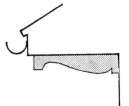

Fig 71
Victorian bracket cornice
A feature of the Renaissance eaves-cornice was its row of finely-carved brackets or modillions; an attempt to imitate this may be seen in the Victorian eaves-cornice with its wide boarded soffit supported by attenuated shaped brackets cut out of wood

The Mid-Victorian style seems to have been accepted by the Classicists but left the medievalists still firmly holding what they regarded as a patriotic front. Their principles were becoming transformed into a trend—undoubtedly a reaction against the rapid spread of Victorian industrialism.

The pace of the industrialists' juggernaut seems to have produced a psychological reaction amongst certain classes of the intelligentsia—artists and the like—so that while the more ponderous types of building were being involved in the Gothic-Classical conflict, the ordinary homes of middle-class people were being nursed by a special sect of the architectural profession. Socialism and the trade unions seem to have been interested in a breakaway movement, for which the active publicists were William Morris and the Pre-Raphaelite mystics. It was a kind of cottage-industry brand of architecture which at the close of the century was represented by the Art Workers Guild. Its provenance was the valleys of Cotswold; many of the gentler architects sympathised with it and were able to affect even large projects to no small extent.

The basic architectural principle involved was anti-Renaissance though not entirely so when it came to detail. And it arose from the same kind of patriotism which had inspired the more important Gothic Revival. Above all, it aimed at separating architecture from the influence of industrialism and attempting to revert to the practices of the Tudor wrights. Thus its most important achievements were in what was known as half-timber.

Henceforth, houses in the country—and in the suburbs of large cities—were to be built in a new kind of country-house style. Plans were more or less Victorian; there was no casting backward as far as the manor house with its obvious inconveniences, though some large houses produced great halls with mock-Tudor open roofs. Leaded casements came back into use, almost ousting sash windows for good and all—they never recovered their popularity. The style was pre-Armada close-timbering and made full use of imitation jettied construction. Nogging of herringbone brick was popular. Not a Gothic Revival, it was nevertheless an undisguised revival of medievalism.

The closing years of the century found many elderly gentlemen deeply involved in antiquarian research into the past history of their country. Old buildings were beginning to be treasured and restoration projects were everywhere in the air. It was but a short step from admiring an old timber-framed house to trying to build one for yourself.

An important social influence appeared to give strong support to the half-timber revival. It is interesting to note that the Royal Court virtually came to an end with Elizabeth, the nobles and gentry retiring to their estates, taking an interest in farming and country sports, settling down as country squires and finding much closer links with their tenants and even employees than would have been possible in Tudor days.

The long years during which King Edward VII was Prince of Wales established an era which saw the revival of the Court. It was a variety of the milkmaid world of Marie Antoinette, but the Prince's entourage consisted for the most part of rich men—nouveaux riches for the most part. And these began to build their country mansions in what came to be known as stockbroker's Tudor, creating for themselves a Walt Disney world in which curly chimneys rose above steep tile-hung gables overshadowed by carved barge-boards. Within, cavernous fireplaces created an aura of hospitality which at night sent its light through the leaded lights of heraldic windows.

The atmosphere of these houses escaped the dreary pomp of the

Early-Victorian mansions. Opulence was illustrated by good living and in these now discredited houses one might perhaps have detected a return to the cosiness of the medieval manor house as it may have appeared to a local peasantry surveying it from a respectful distance.

Thus at the turn of the century we have English architecture established in a fairly sound position following an ordinance founded upon the Italian Renaissance together with a more patriotic domestic style which had whole-heartedly returned to the old gods of barge-board and bay window. The effect of this reactionary movement was seen in the number of distinguished architects who still gave their vote for nationalism and showed this by designing quite large buildings in native brick, crowned with tall roofs and displaying types of fenestration which would never have been approved by Vignola.

The Industrial Revolution had not been confined to manufacturing processes. Today land is filled with notice boards advertising the activities of building contractors, but we have to remember that until the last century such organisations did not exist; anyone wishing to build had to assemble his own team of tradesmen and supply them with materials. But from the end of the Civil War onwards an important part in the development of the English town was played by the speculative builder who bought or leased land, built houses on it, and sold or leased them off when finished.

The first part of the country to be developed in this fashion was the north London suburb of Bloomsbury which dates from the late seventeenth century, after which time the rest of the London suburbs grew up under the aegis of the speculative builder, even such rich districts as Belgravia and Mayfair coming into being at his call. The plan followed was to build complete terraces of single-fronted houses three or four storeys above ground level, with two rooms on each floor and a tall staircase rising beside them. In London the new roads were raised to facilitate drainage, which resulted in the lowermost storey becoming a 'basement'.

True cottages—not those farmhouses which have come down in social status—did not appear until rich and well-disposed squires of the eighteenth century built them for their farm-workers. With the coming of the Industrial Revolution, vast areas surrounding manu-facturing towns began to be covered with long streets of tightly packed dwellings built as quickly and cheaply as possible to accommodate thousands of workpeople brought in from the countryside, many of them probably coming from hovels of unimaginable squalor and glad to be housed within brick and beneath tiles. By bringing their rural squalor to such overcrowded ant-heaps they created the slums.

The skill and efficiency of the speculative builder enabled him to build at low cost houses which could be let at low rents to the working people of country towns, employees such as clerks, shop and workshop assistants, public servants and so forth. During the nineteenth century such accommodation took the form of rows of terrace cottages, single-fronted and two or three storeys high, some with small front gardens, many entered directly from the street.

Passing away from the centre of any country town the traveller will usually be able to detect its rate of growth along whatever street he may be following. First come the narrow twenty-foot plots with tall gabled houses, many of the ground floors of which have been converted into shops. Then come the longer seventeenth-century double-plot houses with roofs parallel to the street and here and there a massive chimney stack. Then come the eighteenth-century houses for pro-fessional men—the doctor, the solicitor—each with its central doorway, perhaps with a porch, and sporting 'rabbit's-ears' chimneys. Somewhere there will be a terrace of nineteenth-century working-class houses, some of rubble stone if such is procurable locally, others of cheap brick, perhaps of the yellow variety. Lastly, as the houses begin to thin out towards the countryside, are the villas of successful tradesmen, business men, or commuters to some large town nearby. These are mainly of the nineteenth century—plain Victorian, Italianesque, or 'stockbroker's' half-timber, 'standing in their own grounds' and dignified by gravel drives winding through shrubberies.

Much of the nostalgic architecture of the Late-Victorian era had been of purely medieval inspiration, but towards the end of the century

attempts were made to 'modernise' the style to form a kind of 'free
Gothic'. This was not, however, a success, partly because all such
efforts were effected in red brick. It had more success across the
Atlantic where it was used in attempts to create the popular country-
house atmosphere so much admired by North American visitors to
Britain.

Faced by fearful population problems on restricted sites, the
Americans had begun to develop an entirely new style of architecture,
the giant steel-framed skyscraper. No style of architecture hitherto
experienced could be employed in these immensely tall structures. Yet
some of them were designed to follow the tradition of the great Gothic
towers of the past and their architects displayed both skill and devotion
in doing so. They may possibly be regarded as the noblest towers
architecture has ever known. Others, however, made little attempt at
architectural expression and appear as piles of storeys presenting a
mere grid of openings in their elevations, an indication that for them
elevational architecture had completely broken down. This presented a
very serious threat to the re-establishment of European architecture,
already reduced to a state of uncertainty and now dealt a shattering
blow from the richest country in the world.

If architecture was to survive when presented with an immensely tall
building, it was necessary at the outset to prevent the design from
deteriorating into a mere pile of identical storeys. This was the challenge
that has never been met. England was at the time fortunate in that a
height limit of eighty feet excluded the towering extravaganzas of
America. But the challenge was only just over the horizon, and English
architects should have begun to study how to check the threat of
'stacked' elevations in order to preserve that basic element of verticality
which elevational architecture demands. For architecture is essentially a
vertical art, every building forming a vertical punctuation of the ground
upon which it stands, serving as a symbol of human effort and always
pointing to the sky. The skyscrapers were themselves vertical monuments of tremendous scale. But with their elevations deteriorating to
such an alarming degree, those of lower structures began to follow suit.

The nearest approach in England to the architecture of American big business appeared in the street front of the multiple store. In the early years of the twentieth century we find architects designing imposing frontages to these, displaying a kind of Hellenistic style, proudly mercantile yet with nothing mean about them.

A dignity had settled upon English architecture during the first decade of the century. It was this era which produced one of the world's great architects, Sir Edwin Lutyens, whose fate it was, however, to display his noblest designs in a distant land.

Under the auspices of the Royal Institute of British Architects the problem of architectural education was eventually taken in hand and set upon a firm foundation. The general acceptance of Renaissance as a national monumental style made it possible to instruct in its ordinance and also to examine and expound the basic rules governing architectural composition. Students of architecture now had to prepare designs and submit them to knowledgeable criticism, often by practising architects who gave of their time—as do members of the medical profession—to help the teachers. Before becoming qualified, all students had to pass an examination in architectural design.

Architectural education, based as it was upon the established ordinance of the Renaissance, could take no account of the rural experiments of the arts-and-crafts movement. Nevertheless, the lure of 'half-timbering' remained as popular as ever for small houses, not only in the country but in the suburbs as well. Such being barred, however, to the trained architect, he had to rely upon English vernacular Renaissance—in other words, the Georgian—for his smaller domestic commissions. Thus Georgian became the officially recognised architectural style for the smaller building.

With the development of new suburbs, the housing estates founded by speculative builders were multiplying. The homes provided were all of the imitation half-timber, tile-hung, bay-windowed type with a sheltering porch—indeed they included all those features which had long represented to the Englishman his ideal cottage home. Such architecture was capable of enough variation to enable the early

H

twentieth-century building estate to present at least something of the impression of a country village.

Into this happy little world of completely 'non-U' architecture, officialdom celebrated the end of World War I by making a monumental miscalculation. For government-sponsored 'housing schemes' appeared, and these were of course all in the official Georgian. The domestic architecture of the eighteenth century forms one of England's greatest achievements. But set miniature squires' houses together in a housing rookery, and the result is not only aesthetically disastrous but creates a demonstration of massed officialdom in the shadow of which no one wishes to live.

The result was a tremendous reaction in support of the irreverent speculative builder—whose prestige in respect of house design has survived his complete switch from the village architecture upon which this was founded towards the new fashion for what is incomprehensibly known as 'contemporary' architecture. So the old gods have at last been banished, and in place of tall gable and bay window the old village street is being insulted by concrete boxes gapped with plate glass.

Much of this latest phase is due to an influence we have met before in English architecture, when the Italian villa reared its campanile above the shrubberies of mid-Victoria. This is the desperate urge to escape from the English climate and the pathetic belief that this can be achieved by building for the sun. We see the 'sun-trap' house advertised . . . but where, alas, are we to find the sun to trap? And building a house from a design prepared in Florida or California may disappoint the English householder as he gazes out through vast expanses of 'landscape' windows upon the rain and frost of an English winter.

Another example of xenophilia is the modern craze for the 'ranch-house', the low bungalow with its broad roof flanked by a massive chimney stack built of rough blocks of moor-stone. This is of course a product of television and its reproductions of a long-established entertainment featuring the hard-riding heroes of the horse-opera. Close study will reveal the fact that they never rode forth unless the afternoon sun was shining. There is magic, too, in the adjective

'Texan' . . . conjuring up visions of exotically attired men and girls
sipping dry martinis round a fire of blazing logs in a cavernous fireplace—which the English house-builder may at least possess.

Not so long ago, the Americans were casting envious eyes upon the
old country houses of England, copying them, buying them up, and
even transporting them across the sea. Now the English, with the
ranch-houses, have reciprocated. But the English house had something
which American wealth could not buy—the true patina of antiquity.

The ranch-house is, after all, merely a large shack or hovel, such as
the English gave up using, apart from the very poor, centuries ago.
Until provided by a benevolent master with a two-storeyed cottage
constructed by a builder, the English peasant lived, ate and slept on the
bare earth or a layer of straw or fern laid upon it. The first people to
sleep on an upper floor in England were those who had learned to do
so through Byzantine civilisation and they established a custom which
continued among their successors until it had become a status symbol,
like white bread, to abandon which would appear to many people a
relapse into barbarism.

Englishmen who went to live in India, however, under the aegis of
the East India Company, found the whole country living at ground
level except for rajahs and nabobs who built palatial many-storeyed
homes. The ordinary house of the country was the bungalow. It is
interesting to recall that by introducing the bungalow into England the
ex-colonials were setting the clock back a dozen centuries and more and
reviving the houses built by the Romans in colonial Britain. The rooms
of these villas were set side by side in ranges, sometimes augmented by
wings, circulation about the house being achieved along covered ways
set against the external walls, which were in fact verandahs.

The bungalow returned to Britain as a result of certain elements of
the population deserting their harsh climate to enjoy one of tropical or
sub-tropical geniality. The colonial type of bungalow which retired
officials and service personnel brought back with them was surrounded
by a verandah which formed its characteristic feature, the builders
unwilling to abandon such a treasured reminder of sunnier, happier

days, again evidence of the eternal striving to try to forget the English winter. The strangely exotic verandahs (Fig 72) surrounding so many Regency houses provide yet another feature of the era which seems to have been happily contrived architecturally.

Fig 72
The verandah
Officials retiring from Indian service to southern
England were inclined to display their nostalgia
by surrounding their new homes with verandahs
having roofs curved in Oriental fashion

Of course instead of sheltering the English bungalow from a torrid sun the verandah in fact took most of the meagre English sunlight from the windows, so that many verandah roofs had to be provided with skylights. Many of the roofs were curved in oriental style, the same curvature being seen in other secondary roofs such as those of porches. Orientalism again creeps into some of the trellised sides of Regency porches, many of which, alas, have all too soon rotted away.

During the Regency period the cottage—in its true form as a small house erected by a builder—appears as a kind of plaything of the rich. At the gates of the Regency mansion is a stylish lodge for the gatekeeper. Set deep in the countryside, the *cottages ornées* or love-nests scattered around the hinterland of the watering-place are similar pleasantries whence wealthy families could indulge in the new fashion for sea-bathing.

At the beginning of the present century the bungalow was still primarily associated with the seaside holiday home. Becoming respectable it was also sought after by elderly retired folk not wanting to be bothered with stair-climbing. Now, as a TV 'ranch-house' the bungalow has achieved an entirely new place in architecture as a status symbol.

Architecturally speaking, it is nevertheless a hovel. Its lines lack that element of verticality which distinguishes architecture. It clings to the ground line instead of rising from it, and only really looks well when seen through the trunks of royal palms which break up its overlong lines and anchor it to the landscape. So far, however, no one appears to have tried to import suitable trees to form a setting for his bungalow.

CHAPTER FOUR

FEATURES

THE DEVELOPMENT of the design of a building under architectural direction occupies three main phases. First there is the plan of the accommodation and of the structural arrangements covering this. Then there is the elevational composition with its array of individual features and the system by which these are arranged. Lastly there comes what is called the 'detailing' of each individual feature; it is these features which by changing and developing through the centuries provide much to interest students of architectural history.

In medieval times all permanent buildings were well-constructed by skilled and experienced masons and carpenters. Thus at any particular period their features were all much the same except in regard to richness of embellishment which of course varied in proportion to the importance of the building and the finance behind it.

Although the great works of the carpenters have perished long ago, some of their features survived without alteration in humbler buildings for far longer than one might have supposed. One of these, the tree arch used for doorways, is formed of a section through the lower part of a tree, split down the middle and the two halves turned upside down and set against each other to form a crude arch. It can be combined with a lintel; shaped to a great variety of silhouettes the tree arch may still be encountered in buildings of seventeenth-century date. In some small buildings, even windows are framed up in similar fashion.

The normal Gothic arch seems to have some affinity with the tree arch and even more with the mighty arch of the cruck. The pointed shape of the latter may have played a part in raising the silhouette of the arch out of its original semi-circular form, but the two constructional systems are so entirely different that it seems unlikely that they are otherwise connected. The stone arch, however, used for spanning openings wide and narrow, is met with in masonry work above doorways and windows.

These two features, the doorway and the window opening, represent the basic details from which the medieval elevation was composed. One structural feature, however, also formed in dressed stone, is of sufficient importance to be regarded as of architectural quality. The weakness of all stone buildings being their angles, from which stones might drop out, special treatment was always accorded these points in the structure. During the twelfth century the quoins or corner stones were often doubled, especially when the walling was of rubble, so as to increase the stability of the angle; this doubling treatment gives a surprisingly strong appearance to the angles of some of the King John's houses.

In buildings of importance the whole angle was often thickened out to form a projection, sometimes in order to accommodate a circular stair. This is called a clasping pilaster (Fig 73a).

In the thirteenth century the two lines of walling meeting at the angle were projected beyond this to form a pair of buttresses set at right angles (Fig 73b). It should be noted that despite their designation they did not in fact perform any abutment duty but were only ornaments to the angle and were often arranged along the walls as well. From this time onwards buttresses began to be designed to decrease in projection as they rose by means of 'set-offs', and all buttresses of the future were so built. Even the smallest buildings had their angle treatments. Any building being raised by a builder who had to be paid for it became automatically a building of architectural importance and had to be so presented.

After the end of the thirteenth century the pair of angle buttresses gave place to a single one set diagonally on the angle (Fig 73c), and this

arrangement superseded the old paired features until late in the fifteenth
century when small versions of them were arranged not at the angle but
near it, leaving the angle itself still visible (Fig 73d). Angle treatments
are usually features of manor house porches; they are often crowned by
pinnacles.

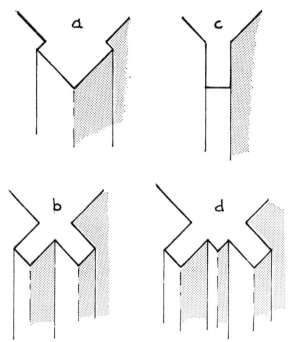

Fig 73
Medieval angle treatments
(a) Twelfth-century 'clasping pilasters', (b) thirteenth-
century pairs of 'buttresses' set at right angles, (c) the
so-called 'French' buttress common to buildings of the
fifteenth century, (d) the form often employed at the
end of the medieval period

Anyone interested in a study of medieval architecture will soon
realise that manor houses, castles, palaces even, were but scourings
from the great cauldron of Gothic glories which had been primarily

intended to provide embellishment for the great churches of the era
and that comparatively few of them filtered down into contemporary
domestic architecture.

The glory of a cathedral or abbey church was the row of arches
which swept down either side of the building from west to east. The
form of these arches, rising from tall pillars and each arch acutely
pointed to add to its height, is what we think of as representing the
Gothic style. But the tall arch notwithstanding, it is in the detailing of
its masonry that the style detaches itself from the great buildings of
previous eras. It is actually the underside, or soffit, of the arch which
expresses Gothic architecture, for whereas in Roman days this had been
flat and plain, in the Gothic it is richly moulded.

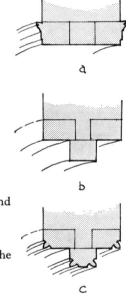

Fig 74
Arch forms
(a) Classical arch with flat soffit and
architrave moulding (see Fig 78)
passing round this, (b) Byzantine
arch built in advancing rings or
'orders', (c) the Gothic arch with the
crude edges of (b) softened by
the use of mouldings

The origins of the change lie—as most architectural developments
will be found to do—among structural problems, in this case how to
facilitate the turning of an arch. All arches are formed by first making a

timber centering and the setting the arch stones around its perimeter; when the arch is locked the centering is struck. The Roman builders had to make a centering covering the whole thickness of the wall in which the arch was set and in this way achieved the flat soffit which in their day was regarded as architecturally proper (Fig 74a).

The Gothic builders arranged only one ring of stones around a much narrower centering, and this 'order' of stones served as a centering for a wider ring above, and so on until the whole thickness of the wall was reached (Fig 74b). This is called turning an arch 'in orders', and from the structural device which it represents the architecture of the Gothic developed.

To have left an arch like this—as the builders in fact did until the twelfth century—would have meant leaving a series of plain arch rings with ugly square edges to them. It was the invention of 'running moulding', developed along these edges to soften them, which created the moulded arch and introduced a richness of style never seen elsewhere in world architecture.

The study of Gothic mouldings brings to one's notice a multitude of elaborate systems of infinite variety. The moulding has two origins. The earliest type is that devised by the masons who cut a 'quirk' or groove on either side of the edge of the stone and rounded this off to form a 'roll' (Fig 75). By adding further rolls separated from the

Fig 75
Mason's moulding
Formed by cutting notches or quirks on either side of the angle and developing these into hollows with a 'roll' between

original one by deep hollows the moulding expanded and joined that formed on a neighbouring edge until no trace remained of the crude stonework, now smothered in the richness of Gothic masoncraft.

Gothic moulding had another and quite different source, this time due to the skill of the carpenter. Most people who use large beams

find it necessary from time to time to shave away sapwood left behind
by the sawyers along the angles of the timber so that only heart wood
shall show. This planing away of the edge left a bevel known as a
'chamfer', which was itself an embryo moulding and could be elaborated
into a hollow chamfer or a wave moulding (Fig 76). These are mouldings
of the days of the late Gothic wrights and do not appear copied in
masonry until that period.

Fig 76
Carpenter's moulding
Begins as a simple chamfer

All Gothic buildings, even domestic ones, were ornamented by
mouldings, even if only chamfers, passing round arches and down the
jambs of openings.

To carry the wide arches of their arcades the Gothic builders used

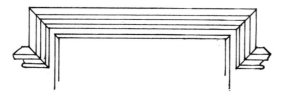

Fig 77
The 'label'
The square moulding always found above seventeenth-
century mullioned windows: it keeps rainwater running
down the wall-face above from reaching the glazing

Fig 78
The architrave moulding
See Fig 79 below. The lowest member of the
Classical 'entablature', also used to frame openings
such as windows and doorways (see also Fig 74)

pillars and these needed capitals to finish them at the top. The type of capital first used was copied from the Roman Corinthian Order which will be described later when we are discussing the Renaissance of Classical architecture during the sixteenth century (but see Fig 81). As Gothic architecture developed, the masons made less use of carvers and turned their peculiar skill at designing systems of mouldings towards converting the *silhouette* of the Corinthian capital into a series of mouldings, thus producing the moulded cap which distinguishes Gothic architecture from any other.

Wide-span arches seldom appear in the ordinary medieval manor house but the smaller arches over doorways are always present and diminutive copies of the great pillars, called shafts, were often inserted into the nooks of the door-jambs, their tops finished with small caps which were copies of the large-scale ones.

The Renaissance represented a complete architectural revolution. An imported style, it owed nothing to architectural history as it had been experienced in England and disregarded this entirely. It had to be learned from scratch.

In order to be able to appreciate the nature of Renaissance architecture one must become familiar with the 'Orders' upon which the Classical styles and the style which aimed at being their renaissance were founded. These Orders, introduced into Hellenic Greece as a system for assuring architectural harmony in buildings of all types, were originally structural but were adapted for decorative purposes by the engineers of Imperial Rome. The Italian Renaissance of the sixteenth century revived the Orders for decorative uses on the elevations of their buildings.

Each Order was based on the use of the column, either structurally or as applied ornament. The columns were usually set in colonnades, connected across their tops by a horizontal band of architecture, the entablature (Fig 79).

The Classical column is divided into three parts of which the main portion is the shaft. This stands upon a base and is finished at the top with a capital.

The entablature, an important feature contrasting with the verticality of the colonnade, is also divided into three parts. The word means 'plankage' and it represents an architectural treatment of what is basically the eaves of the building. Immediately above the capitals is the architrave, which signifies the main beam. The topmost stage is called the cornice, a very important feature of all Renaissance architecture which in fact represents the architectural equivalent of the simple eaves. Between it and the architrave, covering what in a simple roof would be the ends of the rafters, is a flat band called the frieze, which may be plain or embellished with running ornament.

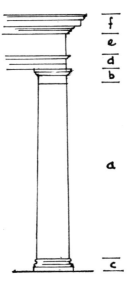

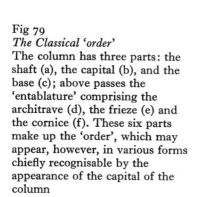

Fig 79
The Classical 'order'
The column has three parts: the shaft (a), the capital (b), and the base (c); above passes the 'entablature' comprising the architrave (d), the frieze (e) and the cornice (f). These six parts make up the 'order', which may appear, however, in various forms chiefly recognisable by the appearance of the capital of the column

These six elements—column base, shaft and capital, architrave, frieze and cornice—make up the Classical ordinance which, although varying in detail with each Order, forms the basis of Renaissance architecture and brings the design of its buildings into harmony with each other— this being the purpose of architectural ordinance.

There is an Order called the Ionic which has a peculiar capital consisting of two large scrolls opposing each other on either side of it.

But in England the Ionic is mainly used in the Greek Revival of the nineteenth century. As far as Renaissance architecture is concerned the Orders to be studied are the Doric—the Roman not the Greek version—and the Corinthian (Figs 80 and 81).

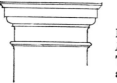

Fig 80
Roman Doric capital
The basis of vernacular Renaissance architecture in England

The Doric capital is of a simple form which can be turned on a lathe, but the Corinthian capital is taller and swathed about with fern leaves out of which uncurling fronds sweep to the angles of the capital. The splendour of the Corinthian capital led to the term being applied to a fashionable gentleman of the Regency period, the designation 'Doric' implying rusticity. A simplified form of the Doric is the plainer Tuscan.

Fig 81
The Corinthian capital
The Corinthian order is employed in the finest buildings

Columns, even if plain without flutes, have to be turned in a lathe if of stone, and assembled with great care and skill by joiners if of wood. But something of their architectural effect may be achieved by the use of flat pilasters which when joined at their tops by a Classical entablature serve to introduce the Renaissance into a design. It is this kind of treatment which forms the basis of the often elaborate door-case which provides the principal feature of the Georgian house-front.

Where neither columns nor pilasters are provided, the architrave, lowest member of the entablature, may be carried down the sides of the opening; this is the origin of the architrave moulding which almost invariably forms part of the domestic doorway of today (Fig 78). Where an arch is employed instead of a horizontal lintel, the architrave is carried round the line of the arch.

We have been discussing the Italian Renaissance as it was created in Italy itself. Its route to England was devious in the extreme. The style travelled to France and to Spain, achieving, in the latter country particularly, splendid architectural monuments. But its progress from France to England was checked by the English Channel, today a busy thoroughfare to the Continent but during most of English history a moat, only to be crossed by armies of invasion. The Anglo-Saxons had come to Britain across the North Sea, bringing with them the culture of the Byzantine Empire through its western capital at Aachen. Great East Anglican ports such as Dunwich or Orford, long vanished beneath the waves, were the entrepôts through which England's wool trade with Europe passed. English contacts with the Latin part of Europe were constantly bedevilled by political or religious strife, and in 1587, when the last Venetian argosy to England broke up on the Needles, the English were busily raiding Spanish fleets whenever they could find them.

Thus when the Renaissance at last reached England it had to be across the North Sea, ballast, as it were, in wool-fleets returning from the Low Countries. These had no architecture of their own to speak of, but were absorbing the splendid Renaissance of Spain, then holding them in thrall. Architecture suffered greatly during the journey; the Renaissance of the Netherlands arrived with convention missing from its ordinance and soon, in the hands of the Lowlanders, became unrestrainedly grotesque. This was the Renaissance which arrived in England, in great force, during the second half of the sixteenth century.

Some of the most impressive achievements of the Spanish architects had been the elaborate frontispieces with which they embellished the entrance doorways of their palaces. When these designs arrived in

England through the Netherlands they became entangled with oriel windows and other delights treasured from the Tudor tower-porches, the whole pot-pourri producing fantastic creations displaying a wealth of sculptural ingenuity but no recognisable architectural ordinance.

The entrance porch is essentially an English feature, required by the rigours of the climate, as discussed earlier. The doorway of the smallest church and even the most humble farmhouse was almost invariably provided with this essential defence, which in the case of the medieval hall became an entrance feature of architectural quality. At first it was a cavernous affair, spacious and welcoming (Fig 82a) projecting well away from the wall of the hall so that its flanking walls would keep side-winds away from the hall-door itself.

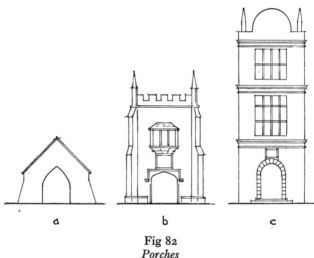

Fig 82
Porches
(a) Simple medieval porch, (b) late-medieval tower-porch,
(c) Elizabethan porch-tower

During the fifteenth century, after the architectural resources of the parish church had been employed to provide an imposing entrance feature, the porch was raised in the form of a tower thus bestowing upon it the architectural quality of verticality. The first floor above the entrance, away from the dampness of unpaved ground floors, became a muniment room for the storage of parish records (Fig 82b).

By providing the porch room with an oriel window similar to that lighting the great chamber at the other end of the house, the tower-porch of the manor house began to assume considerable architectural dignity making it worthy to be regarded as a monumental entrance feature, and it was at this stage that the Anglo-Netherlandish exponents of Spanish Baroque took over with such remarkable results.

The piled-up extravagances which are the Elizabethan frontispieces represent no architectural ordinance and are almost certainly the creations of medieval masons of very great skill and experience trying to reproduce the elaborate achievements of great Spanish architects entirely from inadequate descriptions given to them by English laymen who had received them from Dutch merchants. But with the arrival on the scene of the English surveyor-architect having a professional responsibility the situation changed. For a start, these men would have banned every medieval feature and pared their elevations clean of oriel windows, buttresses, pinnacles and the like. They would then have divided their elevations into tiers of 'Orders', each tier comprising an entablature supported by pilasters of the simple Doric form. Any arches would be semi-circular as in the days of Imperial Rome. That most imposing feature of the Classical entablature, the cornice, would be made full use of at eaves level. The roof-pitch would be reduced as closely as possible to Mediterranean proportions and as much of it as possible hidden behind a parapet. With lead roofs now coming into use, it was often possible to replace the medieval roof altogether (Fig 82c).

But such an essentially English feature as the porch, unknown to the Classical era, could never have survived for long after the submergence of medieval England beneath the waves of the Renaissance. The removal of the porch and the presentation instead of an impressive looking but entirely useless Renaissance door-case would have removed from the house-front its atmosphere of hospitality and doubtless infuriated many a guest waiting before it in pouring rain. To provide shelter for the visitor the English architects of the later seventeenth

I

century devised a peculiarly English feature, the door-hood, a projecting roof carried out from the wall on a pair of brackets. This is not only an entirely English feature but is also the principal manifestation in England of that important Continental style of architecture, the Baroque. And in its humble vernacular form the bracketed door-hood forms an ubiquitous feature of the village streets of England.

There can be no doubt that during the seventeenth century the Renaissance style of architecture, dispensed by English architects in accordance with rules which even at that early date were being published in printed textbooks, had entirely replaced the traditional Gothic and become accepted throughout the land. But a feature omitted from a style of architecture imported from a region with a more amiable climate was bound, sooner or later, to be restored. So, as a diminutive of the Classical portico with its rows of columns, the door-hood was projected farther from the face of the wall above the entrance doorway, its two outer angles carried by a pair of miniature columns or pillars of Doric or Tuscan form. While the largest mansions were able to display the many-pillared portico, the diminutive version with the pair of pillars became the characteristic porch of the English Renaissance. The great portico, however, emigrated during the latter part of the eighteenth century to America where, being transformed from stone into timber, it was forced to change its proportions and employ a slimmer form of pillar. Added to a timber house of gleaming white-painted clapboard, the pillared portico became the splendid feature of the style of American Renaissance known as Colonial.

The pillared porch remained in English architecture. During the Greek Revival of Victorian days its pillars became massive Doric columns, a challenge to some of the Regency Gothic porches whose pillars had been designed as clustered pillars like those of churches. During the 'Chinese Chippendale' period, dainty little porches of trellis-work were fashioned, later to be copied in hundreds, with cheap mass-produced trellis, before cottage doorways, soon to be covered with honeysuckle, wisteria and clematis.

The house-porch, utilitarian, welcoming and essentially English, can still be provided today at negligible cost, its pillars reproduced in spirit by a pair of fir poles or even steel tubes. Anyone passing along a village street will find few doorways that have no porch before them. For a house without a porch is like a face from which a major feature is missing (Fig 83).

Fig 83
Aesthetics affected by sentiment
The sentry-box shaped porch (b) does not appear as welcoming as the broader-proportioned medieval porch (a). Thus proportions, and through them aesthetics, may be affected by pure sentiment

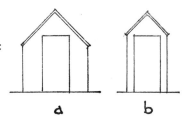

Interesting features of the opulent Late-Victorian era are the conservatories, some of which are attached to the house so as to provide entertainment in wet weather. Derived from these are humbler copies built on to cottages, especially in the south of England where they are sometimes large enough to be used as sun-rooms. In the South-West such rooms are often set before the front door and thus become sun-porches.

During medieval days windows were kept very small and insignificant owing to the scarcity of glass. The first important window found in domestic architecture is that in the front gable of the King John's house which lit the solitary bedchamber. At first it was a small two-light window with a round arch over it such as could be seen in the belfries of church towers, with the difference that instead of a small colonette separating the lights there was a proper mullion so that they could be glazed. Later it became a complete Gothic window though still quite small. During the fifteenth century it was set out on a moulded or carved bracket to become an oriel window, an arrangement repeated in the timber houses of the period.

The great hall of the later medieval manor house was lit by windows similar to those of a church, ranged along the front wall and sometimes the rear one as well. It was customary to make the window lighting the dais larger than the others; even in quite small halls this custom of indicating the upper end of the hall was maintained. It was due to this custom that the projecting bay window came to be developed, a tall feature filled with heraldic glass and very much the status symbol of the Tudor magnate; the end windows in the front wall of the cross-chamber were similarly emphasised by means of good windows.

Shorn of its Gothic detail and reduced to a mere panelling of mullions and transoms, the hall bay continued to appear on the front of the Elizabethan mansion. As the hall of the period was only the height of the ground floor, the bay was carried upwards, however, to light the chamber above, thus sustaining the same tall appearance externally. With Renaissance symmetry demanding the repetition of the bay at the opposite end of the façade of the house, the special significance of the bay became lost while it continued to play its part as a splendid feature of English domestic architecture.

Indeed, the interest and dignity of the lofty bay window led to its being employed for purely architectural purposes, repeated round the perimeter of the mansion, joining with the great chimney stacks in supporting that sense of verticality which is such an important element in fine architecture, especially if the building should tend to sprawl upon its site.

The bay window, both in its tall form and reduced to a single storey in height, refused to be deterred by Renaissance influence and maintained its popularity as a special English architectural feature right through the Georgian era. All-round vision from within the house must always have been popular with the women residents. In the normal Continental house this was provided by the projecting balcony; in the English climate it had to be a bay window. It is only in comparatively recent years that this has been omitted, on the score of cost, from the home on the housing estate.

The normal fenestration of the seventeenth century is achieved by mullioned windows of two or three lights filled with leaded glazing, some of which opens in iron casements (Fig 84a). The lights are rectangular, the Late-Gothic arched head having ended, approximately, with the reign of Henry VIII. It is the Elizabethan window which, translated into joinery, became the farmhouse window of the future, continuing in use throughout the Georgian period where the farmer could not afford the expensive new sashes, and actually outliving the sashed style as the reaction towards medievalism drove it away and brought back the casement.

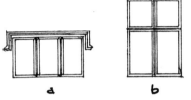

Fig 84
Seventeenth-century windows
(a) The universal mullioned casement,
(b) the cruciform window of the
Stuart era with its high transom

The stone-mullioned window always has above it a straight moulding called a label mould (see Fig 77) brought down for a short distance on either side of the window and there 'stopped'. It is provided to keep the rainwater that runs down the wall-face above the window from continuing down the window glazing.

Until the Elizabethan era, the windows of small houses were filled with wooden frames across which ran a trellis of wattling (see Fig 33). When this was replaced by pieces of glass in lead strips or calms (pronounced 'cames') the same diamond pattern was retained. The lead was probably another item salvaged from the fallen abbeys.

The normal casement window was horizontal in form, divided into vertical lights by its mullions. Horizontal windows being unacceptable in Renaissance elevations, the Elizabethans often raised their casement windows to the vertical Renaissance proportions and ran a horizontal 'transom' across each to reduce the leaded lights to manageable sizes. The transom was usually well below the mid-height of the window so that the lower lights could be made to open with the flimsy iron casements of the period. The Stuart builders raised the transom, increasing the height of the opening casement; this produced the cruciform window peculiar to the first half of the seventeenth century (Fig 84b).

The more important houses of the Stuart period set their windows in orderly rows around the house, their successors of the Georgian period doing the same with the new sash windows. Towards the end of the eighteenth century the Venetian window came into use, its central light arched over and flanked by side-lights half the width of the main window. This was a special window for employment above entrance doorways and at the ends of drawing rooms; as such it was always used singly (Fig 85a).

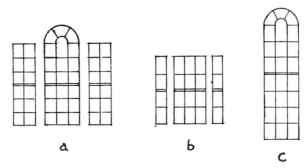

Fig 85
Regency windows
(a) The Venetian window, (b) the 'triptych' vernacular form
of it, (c) the tall staircase window

A simplified version of the Venetian window, a 'triptych' without the arched top, became part of the normal fenestration of the Regency house (Fig 85b). It was square in general outline, in smaller houses even longer than its height, and could not be used in horizontal rows in normal Renaissance ordinance, so the elevational system of houses of the period tended to undergo adjustment with the triptych windows set vertically above each other and not too close together horizontally.

A window which is seen during the Classic and Renaissance revival periods of the first half of the nineteenth century is the 'aedicular' window derived from Hellenic sources. It is surrounded by a moulded architrave mounted upon a heavy projecting sill and topped by a cornice supported upon long drooping brackets curved like those of the

Baroque but set vertically rather than horizontally. Sometimes formed in stone but more often moulded in Roman cement, it is always filled with a sash window glazed with sheet glass and without glazing bars.

The seventeenth century was the period during which even the smallest houses began to provide bedrooms on an upper floor. For the most part these were in the roof-space, where there was space for windows in the gable-ends but where the inner rooms lacked contact with an outer wall. The big Elizabethan mansions were provided with an array of side gables to remedy this deficiency (see Fig 62), smaller houses imitating this system to the tune of a gable here and there.

At this period the enormously tall roofs of town houses in the Low Countries accommodated within these several storeys of bedrooms, all of which were lit by dormer windows framed into their rafters. So the seventeenth-century English farmhouses lacking upper storeys—and there happened to be a large number of these being built at the time in East Anglia—provided roofs into which dormer windows lighting their interiors were incorporated.

There are many varieties of dormer, depending upon the tractability of the roof covering. In thatched roofs we find the 'eyebrow' type (Fig 86a), at first a gable formed by simply raising the side wall to a suitable height to contain the window and sweeping the thatch over it in a gentle curve, the system being converted for use with a dormer by simply raising the window and setting it amongst the rafters.

The Cotswold dormer, which is the diminutive of the Elizabethan side gable, has side 'cheeks' covered with stone tile-hanging or lead (Fig 86c).

The East Anglian builders, always having to cope with the intractable pantiles they were shipping from the Netherlands, balanced the dormer window on the rafters and thrust a short and almost flat length of roof out from the main roof to gather it in (Fig 86b). They were helped with this by the steep pitch of the main roof which had originally been covered with thatch.

During the eighteenth century dormers became familiar features of the Georgian house. Set completely independently in the body of the roof they adopted the Renaissance ordinance, forming part of the architecture of the building and displaying small cornices beneath the edges of their flat lead roofs (Fig 86d).

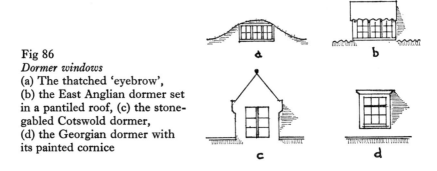

Fig 86
Dormer windows
(a) The thatched 'eyebrow',
(b) the East Anglian dormer set in a pantiled roof, (c) the stone-gabled Cotswold dormer,
(d) the Georgian dormer with its painted cornice

It is a pity the dormer window has gone out of fashion. Always an attractive feature lending interest to the blank planes of the roof, it may be expensive to construct but may be justified by the subsequent saving in the height of the main roof.

The Gothic Revival of Regency days continued to approve of the sash window but gothicised it by giving it an arched head or at least by curving the glazing bars into a reticulated form. The Victorian Gothic Revival toyed with keeping the sash window but was apt to be content with arched openings filled with sheet glass as being less suggestive of the Georgian. But the patriotic movement culminating in the 'arts-and-crafts' and the 'stockbroker' type of architecture rejected the sash window completely, indeed it has never succeeded in making a come-back. In the meantime, however, the casement window had undergone a desperately unattractive modification with the addition of a high transom above which were ventilator lights, generally top-hung (see Fig 104d). No such window had ever before been seen in English architecture and, even though its purpose was to enable the ventilators to be opened when the main casements had to be closed during rain, it has never been assimilated into English fenestration systems and should never be used in an old house. This very ugly window, converted into 'standard steel' was one of the hall-marks of the housing schemes which followed World War I.

If William Harrison, the Elizabethan chronicler who was so astonished at the manner in which house-chimneys were springing up all about him, were to return today, he might be equally surprised to observe the way in which they are all vanishing again. For with the abandoning of the traditional fireplace, once essential to an English home, the tall stack above it has been levelled with the dust.

The fireplace began as a wide recess in the wall, continuing upwards as a wide flue, tapering gradually towards an exit at the top of its massive stack. As the inner wall of the flue, next the room, had to be carried across the wide fireplace opening, the principal architectural feature of the fireplace is always that which bridges this opening. In medieval days it was a wide arch, having little rise, and its great thrust supported at either end by the main wall of the building, for the medieval chimney stack was always planned to project outwards from the wall. With the coming of the internal chimney stacks which were the Elizabethan contribution to house-planning, the chimney arch had to be abandoned as there was no longer any abutment for it. From this time on it was the chimney beam which became the principle architectural feature of the farmhouse interior. Its underside was often moulded in Tudor style, the moulding being carried down the jamb and finished in 'onion stops'.

It is interesting to note that apart from the flue itself these cavernous fireplaces were provided with no special devices for drawing up the smoke. Many must have smoked abominably. Nevertheless there are plenty which due to some happy combination of circumstances draw perfectly against combinations of opposing climatic conditions.

But many owners of old houses will have found that their great fireplaces smoke so desperately as to spoil the enjoyment of logs blazing on one's hearth. For these the writer offers some suggestions—which he has himself followed and found satisfactory—for coping with the problem. For a start the empirical rule may be accepted that smoke cannot be relied upon to rise more than twenty-two inches from its source without being enclosed in a drawing flue. To achieve this situation one may raise the fire-bars, add something below the chimney beam, or set up an internal hood—the first does the least aesthetic damage. The next measure is to treat the underside of the chimney beam so that it presents a feather-edge to the rising smoke—many old chimney beams have already been so treated. The back of the fireplace should slope towards the back of the beam at such an angle that the

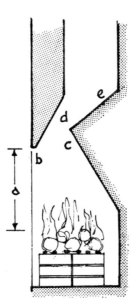

Fig 87
Smoking fireplaces
Some principles to follow for a cure are (a) see that the smoke does not have to rise more than 22in from its source before being engulfed by the flue, (b) see that the underside of the chimney beam is 'feather-edged', (c) see that the sloping back of the fireplace directs the smoke at least 6in above the feather-edge, (d) provide a constricted flue not more than 5 or 6in wide where the smoke enters it (ventura principle), (e) have no ledges with a low angle of rise where smoke may hang and eddy

smoke impinges on this at least six inches above the feather-edge. Where the flue leaves the fireplace it should be reduced in width to no more than five or six inches to create the effect known as 'ventura' and speed the evacuation of the smoke. Within the flue there should be no flattish ledges to encourage back-eddies (see Fig 87).

The fireplaces of the hall and salon which were the principal rooms of the Jacobeans were often very elaborately carved, frequently including overmantels worked into heraldic achievements. A popular form of decoration was the introduction of a flanking pair of male and female supporters, 'Adam and Eve' represented as savage figures and having no lower limbs but emerging from the architecture. These strange manifestations seem to have represented the new interest in colonisation as it spread through Africa and South America.

But all this sculptural ostentation, on the whole foreign to English tradition, survived only as a part of the influences coming out of Spain and through the Low Countries as though to enable the medieval craft of stone-carving to run itself down into final oblivion. For by the end of the seventeenth century the Renaissance style proper came to the fireplaces, making them henceforth plain openings surrounded by moulded architraves to match the other openings such as those of doors and windows. They might be provided with cornices above the opening to serve as a mantelshelf upon which to place china and a bracket clock. A popular moulding at the close of the century was the bulging 'bolection' seen often in panelled schemes.

At the end of the next century the Adam fireplaces appeared with their dainty mouldings—sometimes simply reeded instead of following the true Renaissance forms—and often displaying Classical swags and medallions filled with dancing nymphs. There are Regency Gothic fireplaces with pointed arches and during the Victorian era a variety of fireplaces with surrounds in one or another of the styles around which the stylistic battle was raging.

Every farmhouse fireplace had its oven for baking bread leading out of a rear angle. Closed by an iron door, the oven was heated by burning furze or twigs, the ashes being cleaned out before the dough was inserted. These ovens with their cast-iron doors hinged into frames were products of the industrial era and none can be older than the second half of the eighteenth century.

Logs formed the fuel for the old kitchen fireplace. The far greater heat of the sea coal from Newcastle used increasingly during the Elizabethan era began to destroy the brick or stone backs of fireplaces. This resulted in the mass production of cast-iron firebacks to set against the back wall. Often the designs used were heraldic and might well include crude Arabic numerals, which were being introduced at the time, giving the year in which the casting was made. With the narrowing of parlour and chamber fireplaces to convert them to coal-burning at the beginning of the industrial era, iron interior grates began to appear. The most common type was the 'bird's nest'; its front displaying two arches, the upper of which was inverted and filled with fire-bars. At each side was an iron 'hob', a box upon which food and drink could be kept warm. One of the firms making late eighteenth-century interior fire-grates was the Carron Company—inventors of the carronade— which still exists and is believed to have many of its original designs still recorded.

When the chimney-building boom of the late sixteenth century was at its height the tops of the stacks would end in 'pipes' or 'tunnels' which were often beautifully moulded, sometimes spirally. Many of these charming chimney tops, the last of the successors of the medieval spires and pinnacles which had for long created the English skyline, remain with us today, but some—alas—are being pulled down or covered with cement rendering to save the cost of restoration.

The period of the spiral stacks was of short duration. The stern discipline of the Renaissance drove them away and replaced them with plain square stacks lacking any finish other than perhaps a cornice or a panelled side. In humbler houses the standard chimney-cap of the eighteenth century was a simple brick imitation of the Doric capital with its neck-band or astragal and its cornice-like top (Fig 88c). During the Italianesque craze of the 1840s chimneys became monumental features imitating the wildly corniced and be-bracketed tops of the campaniles (see Fig 70). Today the simple cottage stack with its narrow projecting band—which by the way should never project more than $1\frac{1}{2}$in to avoid coarseness when seen diagonally—can hardly be bettered (Fig 88b). The thick-walled flues of stone chimneys—in the Cotswolds, for example—often have their tops canted inwards to minimise eddies which could cause the fire below to smoke.

Terminal features such as chimney stacks are always important elements in architecture. Always interesting is that diminutive of a tower, the turret. Originating in the projection built at the angle of a church tower to accommodate a stair leading to its roof, the square or octagonal stair-turret became a common feature of medieval domestic architecture. With the coming of the lead parapet gutters, needing constant scouring, the projection of the stair-turret upwards to give covered access to them raised it into an important architectural feature. In particular turrets are found flanking the wide arch of the gatehouse leading into the walled forecourt of the sixteenth century, converting this into a 'frontispiece' and perhaps echoing the treatment of the hall-porch itself.

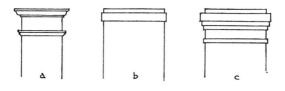

Fig 88
Chimney tops
(a) Cotswold stone chimney, (b) simple chimney band, (c) chimney cap based upon Roman Doric capital (note that projections should not be more than 1½in to avoid coarseness when viewed in perspective)

The emphasis upon verticality so obvious in Elizabethan architecture results in the retention of the stair-turret and, when the spiral stairs became wider, the introduction of a square turret—almost a stair-tower—often set at either end of the central block and joining with the bay windows and massive stacks to create the tremendous scenery of the Elizabethan frontispiece. But with the disappearance of the spiral stair and the introduction of the staircase hall, the stair-turret disappeared.

A notable feature of the medieval great hall was the louvred turret set astride the high roof to carry away the smoke from a central hearth (Fig 58). But with the coming of the wall-fireplace with its chimney stack the roof-turret disappeared, to reappear again as a miniature

Classical temple in the centre of the hipped roof of a seventeenth-century squire's house (see Fig 48).

Throughout the later seventeenth and eighteenth centuries the Renaissance 'tempietto' continued to be popular, sometimes glazed round its sides to give light to a great staircase buried in the heart of the building. On a less elaborate scale it became a feature of the stable block where it carried a clock or at least a bell. Thus what was once an essential medieval feature survived as a pleasant and popular ornament.

One of the gifts of the Renaissance to England was the introduction of Arabic numerals to replace the Roman system of notation. They were employed by house-builders to indicate the scholarship of the owner, being set in a panel showing the date at which his house had been built. They are often very crude in form, the '5' usually appearing as an 'S'. Prior to about 1550 all numerals were Roman—a clue to bogus dating of old houses.

CHAPTER FIVE

ARCHITECTURAL DESIGN

IN THE course of Chapter 3 we watched the procession of English architectural styles, each with a clearly recognisable appearance due to its acceptance of a current ordinance. It is by familiarising ourselves with these that we may be able to investigate the ruins of an abbey or the burnt-out shell of some mansion and decide with ease to what period of architectural history it belongs. But these exercises in the history of architectural style penetrate but a short distance into the full significance of architecture as the most powerful of the arts, producing huge creations of virtually permanent character planted upon the soil of England, buildings into the design of which has gone months of thought based upon diligent study and long experience.

The first requirement of a building is of course that it shall fulfil the purpose for which it is commissioned. This is what Sir Henry Wotton, James I's ambassador to Venice, designated as the First Condition of 'well-building'—its 'Commoditie'. His next Condition was 'Firmness', which is to say that it must be soundly constructed. He quaintly explains that when one is dancing, the building should not dance also— which may be a reference to jettied construction (Fig 11). But the architecture which we see as we pass by should be governed, he considered, by the Third Condition, 'Delight'. It is this Condition which governs the presentation of the building by the owner and his architect to us, the public.

Before the days of the trained, experienced, and professionally reputable architect the appearance of the building had to be left to chance. Thus prior to the Tudor period the appearance of the complete building was not studied beforehand. That it may delight us today is largely fortuitous, and, it must be remembered, due to some extent to sentiment and the dignity bestowed upon it by the patina of history. With the coming of the professional architect, however, this individual was expected to provide some indication to his client of how the new building was going to appear when finished and at the same time make certain that his prophecies were fulfilled.

Before we consider the architecture of a proposed building we must reflect carefully upon the kind of building it is to be. For, practical requirements apart, a treatment suited to a commercial building such as a shop might be less suited to, say, a private house. Even a small public building might be expected to dispense a certain atmosphere of dignity whereas any similar approach in the case of a home might militate against homeliness.

The existing setting for a new building is a factor requiring deep consideration. There is an Egyptian architect practising in Cairo who never sits down to design a new building without first considering the present atmosphere of its surroundings and the manner in which his new design might affect this. He makes numerous sketches of this setting, including the people about it, and then begins to sketch in a new building, fitting it in to the existing scene. Not until he is satisfied that his building will be acceptable to the life about it does he begin to plan his architecture.

No architect should ever insult the memory of his forebears. This refers to the introduction of a new building near an existing one. Here the vital element of neighbourliness has to be considered; an isolated building might be designed in a style which would have to be considerably modified if there should be neighbours to consider. An inconsiderate design may not only offend adjoining architecture but may itself come off second-best in the encounter.

Very demanding is the assembled group of buildings where the design of individuals has to be subordinated to the requirements of the whole scheme. A terrace of houses, for example, must not only be designed as an entity but as a complete scheme with no loose ends (Fig 89)—it was the appreciation of the necessity for this discipline which achieved the noble terraces of the Regency. Although development of this sort is seldom possible today, the principle remains unchanged. The unity of a group should be preserved, while additions to an existing group should be designed so as not to disrupt it.

Fig 89
Terrace composition
A properly designed terrace composition should
always be completed at each end by some kind
of terminal feature

What is undoubtedly one of the most serious defects in architectural design today is the almost universal practice amongst English architects of treating each new building as though it were to stand alone, either deserted in the middle of Salisbury Plain or completely concealed from sight within a concrete jungle. But the land was there first. Its character should be respected. Rural sites in particular have known their trees and their humble buildings for many centuries and would surely beg that these should be respected—perhaps even embellished—by newcomers to the place.

Towns have to suffer the onslaught of progress, yet there is no reason why honest attempts should not be made to help them maintain their historic atmosphere. The European peoples realised the desirability of this attitude when after the last war they rebuilt their destroyed cities, re-establishing them aesthetically along their original archaic lines but with modern planning set behind frontages restored to their treasured appearance. In England the story is a very different one, the blitzed cities being rebuilt to alien forms imported from a new world across the

K

seas. The implication of this is inescapable: the English do not treasure their architectural heritage in the same way as Continentals.

It is strange what little appreciation the city fathers have of the effect of this upon a tourist trade. The present writer will never forget being literally buttonholed by an indignant American visitor who was actually shaking his fist at a new building punctuating unsympathetically the main street of a cathedral city. He shouted that he had paid good dollars to see the old English cities but that in future he would save his money or go to the Continent where they really were civilised and took care of their heritage.

The elevations of buildings in England are nowadays controlled by local government bodies, the members of which have no architectural knowledge. For some time past these bodies have been controlling planning by setting up 'zones'—domestic, commercial, industrial and so forth—and forcing new buildings into the appropriate districts. But since they have taken to controlling elevational architecture they have never considered the creation of architectural zones by means of which they could control the *appearance* of new buildings and ensure that the architecture of each is appropriate to its situation.

This is absolutely vital to the urban scene. The architectural centre of a town should not be ruined by erecting within it buildings of industrial appearance. That the building should be a bus depot or a multi-storey car park may make no difference. If it forms part of the town centre its architectural presentation should be of the highest quality. There is no argument against this unless the local authority is content to accept the ruin of the town centre, which can never be remedied by the erection of any subsequent building.

Two situations, rural and urban, demand special architectural consideration, in both cases inspired by sympathy with the ancient scene. Architecture in the country should be simple. That in the town may be impressive. But both must display the finest quality of design.

Apart from these areas of major architectural importance there are plenty of sites where architecture may enjoy relaxation. There are huge areas of housing estates where adventures in presentation could not only be permitted but even encouraged, in order to redeem the universal drabness which characterises them—incidentally a feature deplored by visiting Continentals. In such regions, variations in ordinance could be allowed, ultra-modern 'contemporary' houses mingling with more traditional designs to satisfy all tastes. For on such sites no harm can be done to existing occupants.

The perfect situation for architectural frivolity is the holiday site where architects and builders can exert their inventiveness to the full in designing houses and bungalows careless of both their own appearance and that of those about them. It could be in such areas that one might perhaps—if it should stop raining—make the best pretence of being in Florida or Copacabana.

These could be the playgrounds of architects. But a *national* architecture, for employment in connection with the most distinguished buildings, or those on the most important sites, is a serious business. It must be broadly acceptable to the public. And it must be able to justify itself in the eyes of the profession to such a degree that any of its members can explain a design to a layman without resorting to mere jargon or abstract platitudes.

In the above pages we have examined what might be described as architectural ethics, the province of the profession. We may now proceed with an investigation into the practical requirements governing the aesthetic presentation of buildings.

Throughout its history, architectural design has been bound up with what we call 'styles' of architecture. Each of these has been founded, followed and developed in different countries at various periods of their history. Some were native-born, others importations from abroad, but each has come to be accepted as a recognisable architectural style the historical development of which can be followed as it proceeds along definable lines. Each style remains broadly speaking consistent, remaining uncomplicated by eccentricities introduced—as in modern times—for the sake of publicity. Each style has, in fact, an *ordinance*, devised by leaders of the profession and accepted by the body of its members.

The medieval builders of England enjoyed a limited ordinance. Prior to the Renaissance there was no organised architectural profession and elevational design was cheerfully fortuitous. Only in the details of features such as doors and windows, porches and towers, does one detect the influence of discipline, fashions changing with the generations but doing so in unison, for this is what is understood by architectural ordinance. Each period had a thread of homogeneity running through it, creating harmony and avoiding clashing discords except when buildings or features of widely separated periods pressed too closely together (an almost unavoidable accident in architectural history which became more pronounced with the introduction of Renaissance work into medieval buildings).

But the medieval manor house, for example, had its widely different portions, the hall and the cross-chamber, joined together without any attempt at creating an elevation. Fenestration was arranged where it was needed with only small regard for aesthetic effect. It is perhaps the naïve effect of this unsophisticated system of accumulating features which helps to reinforce the undoubted charm of the medieval building, almost entirely lacking from the organised architecture of the Renaissance.

No proper architectural ordinance was followed by the house-wrights who raised the closely timbered homes of the Tudor yeomen and merchants. They built walls, roofs and floors in accordance with traditional methods suited to their material. But in doing so they found themselves developing a structural ordinance which being so completely exposed on the face of the building became automatically an aesthetic one.

Nevertheless the presentation of the medieval building remained fortuitous. But when the long-established Classical architectural forms re-appeared at the Renaissance accompanied by a recognised architectural profession, it became incumbent upon the latter to learn how to *design* elevations, that is to say to place each feature of the elevation in a position dictated by a pre-conceived design.

Before the architect could begin to do this he had to study the ordinance of the style upon which his designs were to be founded. He had to learn the details and proportions of the Roman Orders—Doric, Tuscan, Corinthian—for he could not properly introduce column or pilaster without this knowledge. He had to be certain that he could reproduce in a drawing the elaborate cornice by which the buildings of the Renaissance were crowned.

At the coming of the Renaissance England had a host of good house-builders but a mere sprinkling of architects, far too few to have much effect upon the builders' designs. So these continued to build undismayed by the appearance of innovations, merely noting certain basic features of the new style, such as the tall rectangular windows and the wide eaves-cornices, introducing these where they could. It is interesting to note that their vernacular retort to the elaborate cornice was a broad plaster cove set beneath the deep eaves of the rustic thatch, a concession to the Renaissance and unknown in medieval days.

A new social revolution had come to the assistance of both architects and builders. Although printing had been employed for some time to assist the dissemination of knowledge, progress with the craft had been very slow, at first through mechanical problems, but during the seventeenth century partly because of control by a suspicious Establishment. During the next century, however, after licensing restrictions had at last been removed, textbooks on architectural building practice came into circulation and were being widely used by house-builders. Such publications were well illustrated and provided valuable assistance with hitherto only half-understood Renaissance details as well as delineating the constructional systems required to produce them.

Such practical assistance, taking the place of education or apprenticeship, is essential if an ordinance is to be established. The two medieval styles, the masonry and the timber-framed, were too primitive to have known serious architectural control—it is probably by reason of the careless freedom displayed in their use of features that these styles, especially the latter, have more than once been revived.

But it is only in primitive architecture that absence of ordinance can be tolerated. Since the coming of the Renaissance architectural discipline has become a sine qua non. At the present time we can observe

architects flouting this fundamental rule and thereby creating architectural chaos. The good architect is not one who invents something
new, for innovations are more likely to hinder legitimate architectural
progress and bring it to a halt. Progress can only be achieved by
development considered and agreed by a majority of the governing
element in the profession. Unilateral innovation is totally hostile to
discipline. The great architects of the past were those who wrought
splendidly within the compass of the law.

Ordinance, that system of rules by which the architectural 'style' of
a building is controlled, represents an abstract notion transposed into
concrete form and illustrated by the actual lines and details of the
finished product. The layout of an architectural elevation has to be
worked out after consideration of rules of design. These are independent
of ordinance, being rules such as can affect the design of anything—
textiles or the composition of a painting for instance—involving aesthetics. It will no doubt surprise many people that there actually exist
sound scientific rules whose practical application can influence aesthetic
effects. Such rules exist, are incontrovertible, may be applied to any
branch of art, and have nothing whatever to do with taste.

We have only to consider such obvious irritations as top-heaviness or
a clashing of colours to be able to appreciate something of the rules that
may govern design. 'Psycho-optics' is in fact a wide subject, once
studied by architects but now tactfully forgotten. But we may dip into
it a little in order to discover what aspects of it affect elementary
architectural design.

There are always two main components in architectural design. The
first is the general layout of the elevation—which is of course affected
by the style chosen and its ordinance—the second is its 'detailing'. An
element of the first component is scale. Architectural scale is not the
same as the size of the building but relates to the size of its individual
features. Thus a large building will fit far more comfortably amongst
smaller neighbours if it should display the same scale in its layout,
whereas a change in scale may create instant discord even between
buildings of the same size (Fig 90).

Vertical scale in ordinary domestic building is based upon the human figure, as evidenced by the height of a storey averaging eight or nine feet from floor to floor. Except in the thin brick walls of seventeenth-century houses which have to be thickened at floor levels to cover the ends of the main beams, floor heights do not appear on the outsides of houses. But as the sills of windows are usually established at three feet above these, the vertical setting of the windows indicates the vertical scale.

Fig 90
The importance of scale
Changing scale in the middle of a
street may destroy the rhythm of
the street

Buildings of all architectural periods conforming to the same vertical scale, whether two, three, or more storeys in height, harmonise far more easily than would have been the case had their fronts jumped up and down with changes of floor levels. The early nineteenth-century introduction of gas lighting brought about a change in the heights of rooms to avoid fumes; this can make houses of the period uncomfortable neighbours to older ones. Where changes in vertical scale can be particularly irritating is along street frontages, where harmony can be completely destroyed if the fenestration of the individual houses should jump about in switchback fashion. Any terrace composition would of course be completely ruined by such indiscipline.

Horizontal scale in English architecture has been affected by two main factors, one rural, the other urban.

The timber buildings of early days were set out in building bays divided by posts at distances representing the space required to house a plough-team of four draught-oxen each with a four-foot spread of horn. The sixteen-foot 'pole'—an actual pole cut for the purpose—was the standard unit of measurement in the village. A cord of that length folded twice gave the four-foot yard or 'cord'—still used for measuring firewood. Multiples of four feet are commonly found in the main dimensions of medieval buildings, twelve feet being perhaps the most common width of the building bay.

Then, the fronts of adjoining houses set out in bays of similar widths present a harmonious composition. The narrow streets within the defences of a medieval town were divided up into a series of building plots. Each frontage, twelve to twenty feet wide, may still be recognised today. Their elevations to the street may have been changed, almost with each generation, but behind these possibly unremarkable façades one may still encounter interiors filled with massive timbering of the sixteenth century or even earlier.

Timber towns being desperately vulnerable to conflagrations starting from cooking fires, King Henry II had parliament introduce legislation requiring plots along the streets of London to be separated from each other by stone party-walls—a bylaw enforced to this day.

Generally speaking, the house-front was formed in timber framing, behind which the cross-beams or summers spanned between the party-walls and carried the joists of the upper floor which projected over the street by means of jetties. The same system was repeated at each floor, thus creating the tall town houses of Tudor days.

It will be appreciated that such houses were covered with roofs spanning between the party walls and displaying their gable-ends to the street, stormwater from the roofs being collected in lead box gutters provided between them and discharged through spouts into the street. This produced a street frontage formed of a series of gables. As we pass today through town streets we may still find here and there a solitary gable, survival of the medieval frontage system which was replaced gradually during the seventeenth century and onwards.

By the middle of the seventeenth century it became common practice to join plots in pairs or threes to accommodate the long houses with the central stack. The axis of these houses was set parallel to the street and not at right angles to it, so instead of the gable-end we find the street lined with roof slopes, generally with a heavy seventeenth-century chimney stack rising here and there above them. It was during the Stuart period that the medieval street began to lose its gables and the long roofs began to line it, and during the eighteenth century that the great central stacks disappeared and were replaced by the 'rabbit's ears' of Georgian houses, often awkwardly stuck together above party-walls.

Nevertheless, throughout all these changes the original narrow plots remained as punctuation to the frontage, often indicated by changes of material. And what was more significant, the bays of the fenestration survived all architectural changes, the windows lighting them continuing to do so. They might be rough casements or fine sashes, oriels or Regency triptychs or even plain Victorian sashes, but they maintained their positions along the frontage of the street and thus preserved its harmonious rhythm. During the eighteenth and nineteenth centuries the windows were sometimes set in pairs but in easily recognised combinations which may count aesthetically as single windows.

In a large Renaissance building the fenestration is arranged in regular bays, aesthetic and not structural, along the façade, and contemporary 'terrace' compositions of small houses were frequently designed as though representing a single large house. Care was taken to provide a central feature to the façade and, what was even more important, terminal ones to stop the elevation and prevent its 'running out' (Fig 89), an example of sophisticated design generally ignored today.

Given the basic controls exercised by the length of the building, the heights of its storeys, and the positions of internal partitions which may complicate the sitings of windows, the architect has then to consider how to compose his elevation, firstly upon what basis, and then in what direction to develop from this.

Symmetry is the most primitive form of elevational design. In a truly monumental building it may not only be tolerable but even desirable, especially if part of the scheme should include a monumental approach to an entrance. In such a situation, asymmetry might well cause irritation; it would certainly call for an adjustment of the balance of the elevation, an adventure which only a very skilled architect might survive with distinction.

In the square box-like houses of the Georgian squires, the limits of the elevation are too restricted for experiment so that symmetry becomes the only possible course to take. It is as one descends the scale, that one begins to find symmetry becoming first oppressive, and finally, as it attains the mini-monumental, ridiculous. The elevation becomes, in fact, that of a doll's house, a point that the Neo-Georgian architects of between the wars, happily planning their garden estates, never seem to have appreciated.

Another aspect of symmetry when used on too small a scale is that it may throw too great a strain upon the plan of the house and cause waste of space. This was indeed one of the public criticisms of the architecture of the twenties.

Thus in small houses there is simply no place for symmetry in either plan or elevation and a far better type of design is based upon balanced asymmetry, which is not only more practical but can be vastly more attractive. Balance is achieved by making sure that one end of an elevation does not attract all the attention and leave the other looking like the tail of the dog. This is achieved by the association of features. As the entrance to a house is its chief attraction any side-tracking of this may leave the rest of the building slighted unless a gable, a large window, or some such prominent feature is introduced to provide it with its own dignity (Fig 91). Changes of material may play a large part in the balancing of elevations and can also assist the general feeling of the house-front, a simple illustration of the value of contrast.

 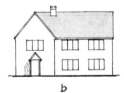

a   b

Fig 91
Balance
Though completely asymmetrical (a) is balanced by
having the porch and gable counterpoised while in
(b) they are joined together to the neglect of the main
body of the house leaving it as an appendage

An interesting example of good balance is found in the elevation of the medieval manor house, where the hall and cross chamber, so completely different in size, form, and alignment, are brought together by the balance of the porch and the chamber gable, with, for good measure, the whole façade centred on the splendid bay window of the hall (see Fig 58). The whole composition is of course fortuitous, for during the medieval period no study had been made of elevational systems.

A knowledge of the rules which govern elevational design will aid the architect but little if he should be lacking in a natural sense of taste. For an elevation designed without obviously ugly features and without noticeable lapses in the more fundamental rules governing design may still look lamentably *dull*. Thus in addition to checking the design for faults it is also necessary to endow it with *vitality*.

It is impossible to place too much emphasis upon the important role played by contrast in the banishment of dullness. It is easy to agree that the occasional introduction of some extra feature in an otherwise plain frontage could give immediate relief to ennui. But does one appreciate without being told that buildings placed end to end look dreary until a single one—or even a gable suggesting one—set at right angles brings a spark of life into the row?

The same applies to the front of the house itself. Breaking the long ridge-line of the main roof with a gable will add to the vigour of the design. A wing, like the medieval cross-chamber, adds delight to the smallest house-front, but tack an addition on to the end of the house and the result may be aesthetically disappointing, for the alignment remains the same and the pleasure of contrast is lost (Fig 91).

An ancient principle of architectural design discovered by the Byzantines is that buildings should if possible gather themselves round a focus. It is for this reason that the long farmhouses of the seventeenth century, gathered round their massive chimney stacks, remain unsurpassed for dignity among the smaller rural houses of England. The box-like houses of the period, perhaps conscious of the vacuum existing between their 'rabbit's-ears' flanking stacks, often set a turret in the middle of the high roof to provide the missing focus.

While symmetry may not be necessary in the smaller building, there are certain disciplinary aspects of cottage elevations which it is well to follow. Ever since the introduction by the Romans of the system of building in bays it has become a firm rule of elevational design that windows shall be sited directly above each other. Only when bay design has been completely disregarded can this principle be ignored, an example being the cottage elevation broken up into horizontal storeys by tile-hanging so that vertical alignment has been lost.

Where the centre line can never be ignored is where a prominent feature such as a gable creates one. A gable-end is a major architectural feature and must always be treated as such. A feature of the present liberal attitude towards architectural design is the practice of splitting up gables into two halves and presenting each of these in different materials ... the architect who offers such a curious device to the public should do so while wearing one trouser-leg in worsted and the other in tweed.

No discussion upon any object of art can proceed for long without someone bringing up the key word 'proportion', usually qualified by adjectives either approving or derogatory but in neither case supported by any kind of explanation. Yet proportion is not an abstract notion but a scientific fact capable of exposition.

Proportion is of course of considerable importance in elevational design. Its purpose is to introduce vitality into an elevation by creating examples of contrast, avoiding indecision and lack of emphasis in the handling of dimensions. Thus a square is duller than a rectangle through lack of contrast between its sides; to carry the idea still further, a pane of glass with its width one-half, or even two-thirds, of its height has obvious proportions and is not so interesting as it might be if its proportions had not been readily spotted. Features appear elevationally steadier if they each have a recognisable axis. The Baroque architects seldom used a circular window, preferring the more stable appearance of the oval *oeil de boeuf*.

Proportion can be affected merely by personal bias. This is especially noticeable in the case of entrance doorways and more particularly porches. A broad porch appears as though embracing the visitor and welcoming him within, while a tall narrow one looks like a sentry-box and except in the case of a small single-plot village home can even appear repellent (see Fig 83).

Broadly speaking, the aspect of proportion to remember is that it should be employed to reflect contrast, the most vital factor in elevational design. The darkness of fenestration contrasts so splendidly with a light wall face—which is the principle reason why it must be so carefully designed. The contrast between the length and height of a building is an example of the significance of proportion. Square fronts can appear dull; in groups of buildings, long façades and lofty ones can be pleasantly associated, to the advantage of both. An area of tile-hanging associated with another of brickwork or rendered walling appears more effective if the proportions of the areas concerned are not easily recognisable so as to injure the effect of the contrast.

Alignment is one of the aspects of contrast which plays a significant part in the arrangement of fenestration. Everyone knows how effective the range of Georgian windows appears on the house-front but possibly few have appreciated that the reason for this is that the row of features is at right angles to the major axis of each (Fig 92a). The Regency

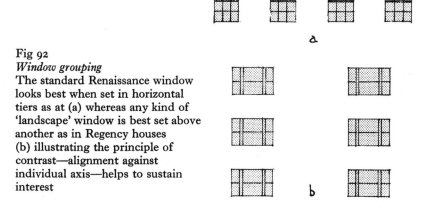

Fig 92
Window grouping
The standard Renaissance window looks best when set in horizontal tiers as at (a) whereas any kind of 'landscape' window is best set above another as in Regency houses (b) illustrating the principle of contrast—alignment against individual axis—helps to sustain interest

triptych cannot be assembled on the same alignment, as its own major axis is horizontal and the effect would be dull, so the sensitive architects of its charming period set this type of window one above the other in vertical lines (Fig 92b).

The over-long lintel formed in steel or reinforced concrete is a feature only comparatively recently introduced into architecture and it has created a type of opening never before appearing for assimilation into our façades. By an elementary rule of design such windows cannot be set side by side, while their great width when set one above the other produces the effect of a complete gap in the elevation.

Fig 93
Dull fenestration
Landscape windows set end to end look boring
and may eventually cut the building into
layers

A recent development in fenestration is to omit all solid walling and cover the whole of the elevation with sheets of material some of which are glass and some painted iron or some other kind of opaque sheathing. This system abandons all attempts to create an architecturally designed elevation.

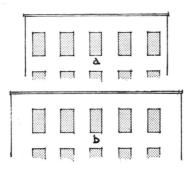

Fig 94
Terminal aesthetics
At (a) the elevation looks
incomplete as though it were
intended to extend it later. The
English Renaissance architects
always closed their elevations
properly as at (b)

CHAPTER SIX

CONTEMPORARY

DURING THE Middle Ages naturally gifted builders, working to no ordinance other than that applying to features, created very many buildings which, even after allowing for the effects of patina and romantic appeal, can still be accepted as successful today. Better organised, but missing the inconsequential charm created by the medieval builder, were the designs created by the first of the English Renaissance architects, who after producing the squires' houses of the Georgian era expanded these into such delightful architectural essays during the too brief adventure of the Regency.

Efficient but somewhat ham-handed were the pugnacious creations of the Victorians, to be softened slightly with the return to the Florentine Renaissance employing unprincipled design techniques resulting in a light-hearted villa architecture not without charm.

The eventual establishment of the Neo-Renaissance, accompanied by a careful study of its rules, and the introduction of a proper system of architectural education, appeared to be stabilising elevational design techniques such as could be taught and examined upon without necessarily obstructing architectural development along orderly lines. But all this was brought down into ruin as a result of two anarchistic movements. One of these was the outrageous creed of functionalism, aimed at the complete destruction of aesthetic architecture. The other was a revolt against the whole principle of observing an architectural ordinance in order to ensure architectural harmony amongst buildings.

The new breed of 'saboteurs', originally working from the European Continent, realising the publicity value of rejecting standard ordinance invented architectural styles of their own and explained that this was 'contemporary' architecture. Lacking both ordinance and rules, however, it could not be regarded as architecture at all. It could neither be established nor followed by anyone, and this included students, so all it achieved was the destruction of architecture—and, what was worse, an end to its historical development.

For more than twenty years, architectural education, in so far as design was concerned, has had to be abandoned for lack of an architecture to teach. The history of architecture is taught no longer, thus traditional design, even the long-admired Georgian, has been forgotten and is now only seen travestied.

The new buildings exhibited two principal characteristics, repetitive dullness and frenetic imbalance. And the spread of anarchy resulted in displays of eccentricity. An 'innovation complex' introduced materials, such as black bricks, which had never been seen before in architecture and harmonised with nothing about them. Every kind of sheer vulgarity was inflicted upon town and country, ancient sites not being spared.

By itself, this extraordinary revolution in an ancient aspect of social behaviour would have been enough to wreck any profession. But a more serious—because more orderly—threat was the development of functionalism, a movement which, to be fair, was not inspired by a desire for publicity, but the result of frustration created by developing constructional techniques employing materials new to architecture. The American skyscraper must have presented a daunting challenge to any elevational designer—though some of them in fact created towers of both dignity and beauty—but such tremendous structures could hardly have failed in the end to hurl all architecture into the lap of the structural engineer.

This belief in versatility of the structural engineer actually resulted in the establishment of an ordinance—not an architectural ordinance but a structural one. Elevations were reduced to bare essentials, with vertical pillars of steel or reinforced concrete and horizontal beams spanning between them and carrying the floors. To keep the occupants of the building from falling into the street, parapet walls three or four feet high were thrown across from pillar to pillar leaving long gaps between the tops of the parapets and the underside of the beams overhead. Thus the ordinance when complete comprised a row of pillars joined by horizontal bands of concrete separating the windows of each storey (Fig 95).

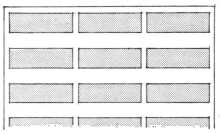

Fig 95
Functionalism
Non-architectural design
based upon modern steel- or
concrete-framed construction

A development from this ordinance is the 'layer-cake' elevation in which the short lengths of pillar are set behind the window glass so that no vertical lines whatsoever are left to the elevation, a deplorable rejection of that vital element of verticality which is the essence of architecture (Fig 96). From this device of hiding parts of the structure behind glass we at last arrive at the complete glasshouse which makes no concession at all to architectural design but covers the whole of the building under a sheath of 'curtain wall'.

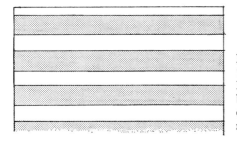

Fig 96
The 'layer-cake'
Developed from functionalism
by leaving out all vertical
elements and retaining only
recumbent architecture

Another style of building—again a product of novel systems of construction, in this case mass-production—which defies all previous

L

conceptions of elevational design is the grid of prefabricated sections similar to those used by children playing with toy building-sets. Prefabrication, usefully employed after the destruction of homes during World War II, is totally unsuitable for buildings of major size and importance, for quite apart from its failure to exhibit even a pretence of architectural design it is so wearisomely dull.

It is elevations such as these which could benefit enormously from the application of one or two of the simple devices known as architectural punctuation. This can take three forms. Horizontal punctuation—which should really be called vertical but its devices are horizontally employed—can extract certain selected storeys from the blankness, and by giving them a little extra treatment enhance both their individual dignity and that of the whole elevation. The ground

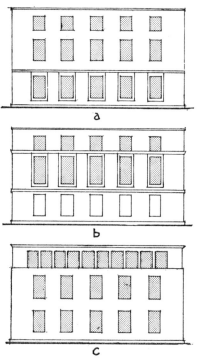

Fig 97
Horizontal punctuation
Adds interest to what might be a dull elevation. In (a) emphasis has been given to the ground storey. The system used by the Italian Renaissance architects was to create a *piano nobile* on the first floor (b). The Spaniards elaborated the most prominent part of the building, its top floor (c)

floor may be selected for treatment but this may be unrewarding in a street where it is seen foreshortened and often hidden by traffic (Fig 97a).

The early Renaissance palaces threatened to appear somewhat uninspiring after the liveliness of the Gothic, but the Italians treated the first floor as a *piano nobile*, a device which added considerable interest to the building (Fig 97b). It was the Spaniards—so often the finest architects of their day—who conceived the idea of making the top storey, most prominent in the distant view, the one to receive the most distinctive treatment (Fig 97c). This device could with advantage be employed today at the summits of some of the more ghastly tower blocks.

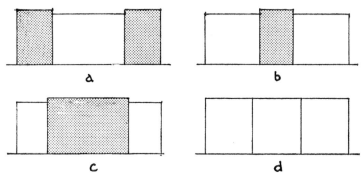

Fig 98
Vertical punctuation
Can break up comprehensive dullness in an elevation: (a) introduces terminal features, (b) a central feature, (c) suggests a central block with wings while (d) suggests a lack of decision and illustrates the error of dividing into equal parts, thus sacrificing contrast

Vertical punctuation—that is horizontal punctuation by means of vertical features—is not difficult to achieve. There are two systems, one of which is to emphasise the centre of the front (Fig 98b), while the other establishes terminals to it (Fig 98a). It is most important that any central division should be clearly presented as either wider (Fig 98c) or narrower (Fig 98b) than one-third of the whole front so as to obviate any sensation of indecision. Terminal punctuation may suggest wings or towers but each must be clearly secondary to the centre division.

The simplest form of punctuation is the nodal, merely a matter of emphasising one of the features of the fenestration. It can be employed centrally (Fig 99a) to draw attention to an entrance below, or terminally (Fig 99b) to bring the façade to a stop at each end.

The eccentricities of the 'saboteurs', jumbled together with functionalist frames, featureless grids, and blank precipices of glass, form what is known today as 'contemporary architecture'. This is a complete misnomer, as an architectural style must display some form of ordinance tying it together into a style. Otherwise it will lack homogeneity, dispense no atmosphere of serenity and merely combine to form a spectacle of chaos.

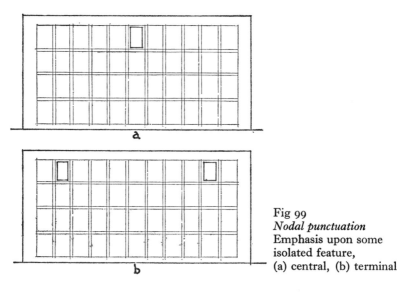

Fig 99
Nodal punctuation
Emphasis upon some
isolated feature,
(a) central, (b) terminal

A certain amount of confusion was created during the last century by the division of the profession into exponents of three main historical styles of architecture, Classical, Gothic and Renaissance. These, and others which filtered in from time to time, did not mix in the least; but there existed a distinct historical precedent, in that the mélange represented as it were an exhibition of architectural development through the centuries, just as though the buildings concerned had actually been contributed during the periods employing the styles they illustrated. They were of course all historical styles and had to compete with no structural or other eccentricities.

Revolts against this confusion were bound to occur from time to time, the 'arts and crafts' movement being one. But far more emphatic than this gentle venture was the 'Art Nouveau' campaign, the theme of which was to omit any architectural feature and any form of architectural ornament, which had even been seen before in any period or style. The artists of the Art Nouveau favoured such improbable models for architectural ornament as vegetation and drapery; their sign-manual was the tulip. They scored heavily over the 'arts and crafts' by designing for mass-production in factories at the end of the nineteenth century. Art Nouveau, being purely revolutionary, was basically unsound, but it was at least an attempt at a new and orderly style of architecture. It could not but fail, if only because of the method by which it was propagated, but after decades of derision it has now become respected for its honesty of purpose.

Nowadays it is the custom to excuse unauthorised innovations by describing them as avant-garde, the thoroughly dishonest implication being that the exhibition concerned represents the advance-guard of a main body of popular approval which will shortly appear in support and overwhelm all opposition. This ridiculous expression should have been discarded long ago.

Bad architectural design may be the product of varying degrees of inefficiency ranging from ignorance to arrogance, more often than not a combination of both. This is true not only of the design of new buildings on isolated sites but more particularly of those required to harmonise with existing neighbours.

One of the scandals of modern times is the licence to create Permanent Discord. An example of this deplorable practice may be encountered whenever some fine terrace composition is broken into at the sale of some of its frontages and the new filling is designed without regard for the survivors. The architect may plead that it was intended eventually to pull down the remainder of the terrace and rebuild according to his design. Meanwhile, however, discord has to be suffered. And it is not unlikely that when more of the terrace is pulled down another architect with his own ideas on design will be engaged. Thus Permanent Discord is assured.

The remedy for Permanent Discord should be that planning committees (and what, after all, are they for?) should insist that the first insertion should take into consideration the harmony of the result, even though this should be considered temporary. The public scene is the public's concern—it is entitled to be accorded harmony in perpetuity.

An arrogant contempt for existing buildings by architects providing neighbours for them is particularly unfortunate when it comes to village sites. The primary element contributing to harmony is ordinance, and certain types of building introduced during past centuries have in their day combined to create a *vernacular* ordinance; in so doing they have planted an indelible image upon the countryside. The most powerful components are the long farmhouse with its central chimney, and the Georgian and Victorian house with its rabbit's-ears chimney stacks. Cottage terraces and even semi-detached pairs may fit in with one or the other in accordance with the arrangements of their chimneys. But the chunky 'shoe-box' or the TV Texan ranch-house will conform to neither of these vernacular ordinances and must remain a discordant element in the rural scene. Such un-English buildings belong to the housing estate or the holiday camp.

A type of roof which has been introduced apparently for no other reason than to express originality is the monopitch, which is simply a lean-to roof with nothing to lean against. It used to be employed in humble structures such as farm buildings where it was usually covered with corrugated iron. As this has a very low working pitch the roof was so nearly flat as to appear reasonably stable. But the new monopitch has the normal pitch required for tiling and may cause one to catch one's breath for fear that it should plunge to the ground.

But even the form of a building may be discordant if it offends against local colour. Indeed in the distant view it is probably colour which counts the most where serenity is concerned. Improvements in transport facilities by canal and railway have enabled supplies of bricks to be introduced into regions which had hitherto built in stone or cob, thus bringing about the intrusion of red houses amongst a majority of cream or grey ones. During the Late-Victorian period, considerate architects made some attempt to restore harmony by using yellow bricks but we can see today that at a close view the cure was found to be worse than the ailment. And now we have a trend in black bricks which harmonise with no other building material known in England.

Until less than half a century ago, architecture was the principal means by which a man of taste could display this to the public. Whatever the interior of his home might lack, it would be a matter of personal pride for him to assure himself that its public presentation was faultless. From the eighteenth century onwards, when the squire was a patriotic man who regarded an Englishman as worth two foreigners, he would certainly have regarded his house as representing the image of his country to visitors from the Continent. This attitude has completely disappeared. The building owner of today is solely concerned with the disposition of its interior—how it suits its purpose and how it impresses visitors entering it. He cares nothing for what he may be inflicting upon his countrymen who may daily have to pursue a shuddering course beside it. One recalls the jingle: 'My face—I don't mind it—I'm always behind it. The *people in front* get the jar!'

Alexander Pope might have been describing the architectural situation in England today when he wrote in the seventeenth century:

'Lo! thy dread empire, Chaos!, is restored;
Light dies before thy uncreating word:
Thy hand, great Anarch, lets the curtain fall,
And universal darkness buries all.'

CHAPTER SEVEN

ARCHITECTURE IN THE FUTURE

THE ARCHITECTURAL—one might perhaps call them anarchitectural— disasters which cover England today are made doubly horrifying by reason of their prominence. The great architecture of the past—of Egypt, Greece, Syria, Anatolia—was raised in arid lands of sand or rock to which a building was a valued asset bringing life to the scene. The English countryside, however, is a beautiful one of hills, vales, woods and streams, in which almost any building may seem to be approaching desecration. It is therefore the first duty of an architect to do his utmost not to spoil, and if possible to enhance, the natural beauty of the site with which he has been entrusted. England is not a country in which to advertise architecture but one in which to conceal it. The writer, after completing a house beside a Wiltshire lane and asking acquaintances what they thought of it, was delighted when the reply came that they had passed it without noticing it.

If one were asked what constituted the basic defect of architecture today, the first thought to spring to mind might be its bad manners. And so many of today's buildings are very large indeed and form inescapable obtrusions inflicted upon a large proportion of the public, permanent eyesores which may have to be endured by generations to come.

Architecture today may demonstrate bad manners in two ways—not only by offending the contemporary public but by slighting the memory of previous generations by ignoring the claims of existing buildings to be treated with courtesy. There is no excuse for instance, for inflicting displays of 'avant-garde' pseudo-architecture upon ancient settings such as medieval universities.

Faced with general ugliness of presentation, we have no chance of appreciating the fact that there are plenty of architects today who can make sensitive use of traditional materials, and hint at archaic ordinances without subservience, to their own credit and in a fashion which complements the old work to which they may be adding. There is no need for a modern building to suffer in the least as a result of its architect having given consideration to its external presentation. Indeed the skilful architect will find it a rewarding exercise to create a modern interior behind a traditional façade. It is not necessary to present the whole exterior of a building in one architectural style. The writer has often employed a 'Janus' technique by means of which he shows one kind of elevation to the public and another to the garden—an old device which used to be known as 'Queen Anne front ... Mary Ann back!'

An architect must see to it that his clients receive the maximum possible sunlight into their houses. But on north elevations he may well find it possible to extend courtesy to some neighbouring old property by designing in something more resembling a traditional style. He can still have his landscape windows at the back of the house.

One of the most desirable changes in policy relating to modern architectural manners is the preservation of the dignity of street frontages which have been maintained without aggression up to a few decades ago.

Architecture could be regarded as three-dimensional poetry. With the introduction by the Romans of the system of subdivision into bays, architecture acquired a rhythm. One cannot fail to experience this when watching the tremendous sweep of the arcades of the Colosseum, or, to a lesser degree, those surrounding the Piazza of St Mark. The interior of a twelfth-century English cathedral has already taken upon itself a rhythm seeming to echo the tremendous drum-beat of 'The Battle of Maldon'. It is this same rhythm which has been perpetuated for so long in the street frontages of the English town. To break it by the insertion of some wide-bay functionalist elevation is to wreck an ancient street (Fig 100). There is no place in architecture for ragtime! And with the accumulation of these monstrous intrusions we arrive at Perpetual Discord.

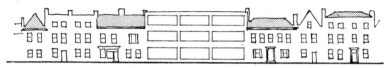

Fig 100
Urban bad manners

Unlike the—possibly happier—countries of the New World, England is saddled with a long history. This affects not only the social attitude of the Englishman but the appearance of the very land itself. Every field—call it a building site if you must—has a history, very possibly illustrated upon the ground. And this visual history of a place, once destroyed, can never be replaced or restored. The English people are undoubtedly the poorer for the loss. Ask an American and he will agree.

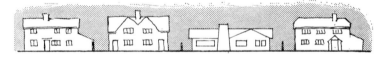

Fig 101
Rural bad manners

To an even greater degree, English history remains alive in the shape of many old buildings in need of preservation. The architect of today, thinking in terms of balsa-wood 'projects' translated into concrete and covered with a syncopation of synthetic 'claddings', may no longer retain any knowledge of even the traditional building methods of England. He has forgotten lime mortar and only uses portland cement with its corpse-like colour and sheen. He has never experienced the mysteries of a stone quarry, known nothing of masonry and the marvel of the dressing of stone on the banker. Before he can be allowed to lay his hands upon some valuable old building he must set aside his drawing-board and go down to the quarry and begin to study his craft anew. He must try to obtain knowledgeable advice upon the weathering of stone and the mystery of the callus which the elements form upon it. He must study mixes of mortar. Above all, he must teach himself true ways of displaying jointing, that the pattern of the stones may remain clear and unblurred.

In addition to the traditional building materials long used in England, there exists today a wide range of synthetic substances, some for use structurally and even more for facing purposes, these last being perhaps more suited for use in those areas where frivolity may hold sway. Many of these are employed to create colour effects. The use of colour in building elevations illustrates a simple aspect of the design principle of employing contrast to create vitality. But in following this practice one should note that colours have optical weights, a factor which may affect their use architecturally. Not only does a dark-coloured wall appear top-heavy above a lighter one, but so does a warm red above a cold blue. And darkness seems to approach one, while a light wall appears to recede. Thus no colour or even tone should be employed without considering its architectural properties.

In sun-starved England the artificial tinting of wall-faces has never played any significant part, the most notable exception being the colouring of limewash on a cob wall to give an effect of brick. Coloured paint for joinery did not appear until the beginning of the last century and, again, was then used to make deal look like oak—graining was a development from this. Experiments with paint are now appearing in attempts to brighten certain dull urban frontages. This needs careful consideration; strong colours should only be employed with restraint and in small areas of building, except of course in the frivolous regions. Pastel shades, however, have great value when applied to rendered walling—the pink cob walls provide a precedent. The panels of what looks like painted iron displayed in so many 'curtain wall' frontages appear on the whole unattractive in urban settings and would seem more appropriate in areas where the preservation of dignity is not essential. The city street is not an appropriate setting for a perpetual harlequinade.

The English roof is a characteristic feature of any scene. Even in towns its steep slopes are prominently displayed; the rather ugly slates usually appear on low-pitch roofs and are often broken up by parapets and chimney stacks, but the tall tile-covered roofs are always visible. Clay tiles, replaced time and time again as winters take their toll, are formed of a material which readily encourages the growth of lichens, and this fact added to the normal variety in tone of the tiling makes it one of the most attractive features of the English scene. But nowadays clay tiles are difficult to obtain, their place having been taken by tiles pressed out of cement and sand. Such tiles are not receptive enough to afford a good lodgement for lichens, so they never acquire that desirable patina which comes from weathering and always remain dull and lifeless and, of course, identical in colour. The best way to use concrete tiles is to select, say, three stacks of tiles which are nearly alike in colouring and scatter tiles from each over the roof to break up the characteristic flatness of the material. In accordance with the principle of contrast the proportions of the mix should be unequal.

The surface texture of a wall-face plays a large part in its tonal value. Natural building materials are essentially rough in texture, thus flatness in the surface of a building looks unnatural. A rough texture such as is produced from a wood 'float' upon external rendering can also assist patination. Fine aggregate, of not more than a quarter of an inch gauge—road sweepings were used during the turnpike era of the Regency—is best for rendering. Pebble-dash is unnatural and the pebbles fall out, while the new sprayed 'Tyrolean' looks messy and in no way suggests a natural material.

Old masonry is of course a delight to encounter, for each of its stones is different and creates an individual patina. The same may be said of old hand-made bricks. Owing to the thickness of the joints of brickwork a very strong pattern is formed and the character of this can make a great deal of difference to the appearance of the wall. The hollow brick walling of the present day is built in 'stretcher bond' with each brick lying along the wall-face. A far more attractive effect is created by restoring one of the old bonds, the 'English' or the 'Flemish' (see Fig 8), by employing 'snapped headers' the ends of which show on the wall face and liven it up.

Mortar is the matrix in which stone and brick is set. It is not meant to be seen except where its edge appears on the wall-face. The shapes of the individual items forming this should on no account be obscured by mortar which has been smarmed anyhow over the joint. Cement is an indelible stain and once it has touched the face of stone or brick the disfiguring scars remain. With the decay of workmanship one may see examples of clumsy jointing, and some of it is so badly executed that there seems to be more cement than stone. Such messes are in no way improved by being scratched with the handle of a bucket. The curious type of ornamental pointing known as 'ribbon pointing', which the Society for the Preservation of Ancient Buildings has been preaching against since the beginning of the century, is still with us.

The covering of ancient masonry with rendering is an admission of final failure. For a portland cement rendering can never be removed and the building is ruined *for ever*.

In addition to the valuable historic buildings, there are hundreds which are not in that category but are nevertheless important memorials of past history. Not only are these buildings equally in need of preservation, but they are today greatly esteemed by people who appreciate homes with a tradition behind them. Chief amongst them are the long farmhouses of the seventeenth century, those imposing residences so many of which were cut up into separate cottages during various nineteenth-century agrarian troubles which forced small farmers to abandon their farms and work for some neighbouring landowner with more capital to see him through.

There are two main planning difficulties to be encountered by architects trying to convert a long house of this type. The first of these is the lack of passage circulation between rooms planned before people troubled themselves about such refinements. The other is the obstructive position of the central stack. During the eighteenth century many of these stacks were cleared away and dog-leg stairs raised on the site to replace the old spiral. But this represented the loss of the house's most impressive architectural feature.

The solution is to build an 'outshot', an annexe passing along one of the long sides of the house. It can provide access to all the rooms in the house, a staircase to replace the old spiral—retained of course as a curiosity—and if prolonged can accommodate bathrooms at either or both ends (Fig 102). The outshot must be added to the side of the

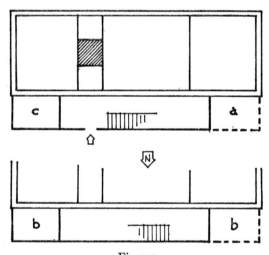

Fig 102
Modernising a seventeenth-century long house
By adding an 'outshot' preferably on the north side and containing the entrance: (c) is a cloak-room, (b) a bathroom. If a second bathroom is required it could be sited above a utility room (a)

house receiving least sunlight in order that full use can be made of the fenestration on the sunny side. This means that the entrance must be in a northern outshot and the garden set before the south front, regardless of the direction of the road frontage. Should it be necessary for the new outshot to face the public view the greatest consideration must be given to the design and materials employed, in order that the atmosphere of the old building may be reflected in the new work.

Turning a house back to front may sound a costly disturbance and the writer has enjoyed many a quiet chuckle when observing the consternation which such a suggestion has produced. But the practical operation may in fact be quite small and when the client has discovered how much sunlight has been let into the house he has often expressed surprise that 'no one has thought of it before'.

More difficult to modernise is the squarish house of the eighteenth or nineteenth century, the obstruction in this case being the narrow stair hall set in the heart of the house. The thing *not* to do is to sacrifice one of the front rooms and make it into a staircase or 'lounge' hall, popular during the second quarter of this century but in fact a perfectly useless apartment around which draughts from the front door conduct an endless battle with those dropping down the staircase.

Fig 103
Modernising a square house
Remove the cross-wall from end to end. On one side form a large living room (a) and on the other a dining room (d) and kitchen (b). The entrance hall can be extended and a cloakroom (c) provided beside it (note that it may be an advantage to turn a house completely about face so as to catch the sun)

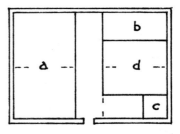

One of the pairs of front and back rooms can well be joined to form a more convenient living room—the cross-wall is seldom load-bearing—while on the other side of the house a little replanning can produce a better dining room with a workable kitchen behind (Fig 103). The cramped stair has still to be tackled and it may well be best to move this into a new annexe built on to the back of the house and containing a new bathroom and cloakroom which will not obstruct the central circulation of the house. Here again it might be in the interests of sunlight to turn the whole house back to front. Many Victorian houses have quite plain entrance fronts which would be no loss to architecture and the transformation of one of these to a garden front before which flowers could flourish in the sunshine could well add to the pleasure of the beholder.

The success of any alteration to a house-front depends almost entirely upon careful fenestration. Perhaps the most infuriating displays of bad taste one can find in modern architectural practice are to be seen when windows are inserted in an existing house without regard for its existing fenestration. This is the nadir of architecture, reflecting a combination of bad manners and abysmal innefficiency. Anyone making such an alteration should study the practice of the past, for the eighteenth-century—or even the nineteenth-century—builder would never have been guilty of the uncouth mutilation of an existing building through sheer indifference.

In these days all architecture, great and small, is bedevilled by high building costs. But far too much attention is being paid to this factor. Excuses based upon it to justify excessively ugly mass-produced architecture are in cold fact seldom valid. And much of the casual damage being inflicted upon old houses may eventually have the effect of lowering the selling price.

The insertion of a single window in an existing elevation involves the same consideration—and probably far more trouble—than did the designing of the original elevation. Mass-produced steel windows appeared during the housing campaign following World War I. They were made up in standard sizes, the idea being to help create a kind of housing ordinance, stabilising its architecture. The standard casement was provided with steel glazing bars forming a grid of approximately Georgian proportions, later rendered ridiculous when the vertical members were omitted under the impression that this would assist the 'contemporary' architectural style towards which architects were believed to be aiming. The ladder-like standard window was a disaster whose influence remains. (It may be noted that Victorian cottage windows are frequently found with horizontal glazing bars only, but designed with their pane proportions carefully considered and not just the result of leaving out vertical bars—see Fig 104.)

The development of the steel window assisted the creation of the huge landscape windows of recent years. Filled with plate glass, these no longer represent designed fenestration but simply areas where the wall has been left out.

Fig 104
Late types of window
(b) is the standard steel window on Georgian lines, after World War I, (c) is the same with all the vertical bars left out, the 'ladder' window with badly proportioned panes—compare this with the normal Victorian cottage window (a), with its pleasantly proportioned panes; (d) the 'ventilator' type of window, invented late in the nineteenth century—though useful it looks uncouth and should never be introduced into an old house

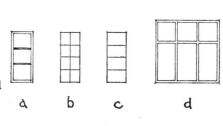

a   b   c   d

One of today's problems is the presence over town and countryside of late nineteenth-century houses planned to accommodate the large Victorian family and its staff. It is certainly pleasant to discover that more and more attention is being paid to the preservation and modernisation of many of these white elephants threatened with the bulldozer. The demand today is that they should be converted into flats, but the writer considers this an unsound practice and has always refused to countenance it. For in buildings having ordinary wooden floors the occupants of the lower flat must necessarily suffer the noise emanating from that above. The garden is either banned to the upper residents or shared uncomfortably between both properties. Often the front door is shared.

The proper way to subdivide such a house is to make it a semi-detached pair. The provision of an extra staircase—its omission being another of those maddening sacrifices to economy—is a small price to pay for superlative advantages, which include easy access to fuel and

M

the proper subdivision of the garden to give each family its own private stamping ground.

The Mid-Victorian house was splendidly constructed and its expansive layout facilitates replanning. While often ugly to modern taste, the ordinance was based on traditional lines and it will generally be found that it is mainly in the detailing that the discredited Victorianism may be displayed. It is not difficult to rectify such minor problems with a bolster or even a pickaxe. The replacement of plate-glass sashes with new ones divided by glazing bars can set a Victorian house back a century in time. It is all a matter of care and interest—a renunciation of the modern professional attitude which inclines to the view that it is best to pull the place down and build a new one. Bricks and mortar are expensive, especially if well laid.

To return to matters of fenestration, it has to be confessed that the Georgian glazing bar is a troublesome harbourer of dust and many housewives prefer the large sheets of Victorian glazing. In casement windows the bars may be omitted, as indeed they often were in the smaller cottages and farmhouses. It is the scale which counts; even a large window may look well in an old house provided it be subdivided into lights of a suitable size to conform with the basic scale of the fenestration.

The irreparable loss of so many old buildings is, alas, a notable feature of our times. What will our children think of us as they discover the survivors and compare them with the formless, faceless 'contemporary' leviathans which obscure their hereditary horizons?

The future of the national architecture of England seems bleak. The profession seems content to defy public opinion and raise its foals of the nightmare in important situations. National architecture—which may include the lack of it—is an expression of the Establishment and under its protection.

One wonders what will happen to the functionalists. Having reduced all building to an expression of the minimum, and stuck to this for half a century, do they intend to continue their strange inertia indefinitely? They might copy the example of the Byzantine engineers and introduce the duplex or triplex bay by providing non-structural vertical members solely for the sake of aesthetics—if such an outrage against the sacred cow of functionalism could be conceived—and thus begin to restore that element of verticality which is the essence of architecture. Such a modification might even become a possible basis for a new ordinance having in it something of architecture.

For the devotees of the grid or waffle type of elevation there could be some hope, if they would only steady these by employing some form of punctuation. Elevations so treated would at least give the impression of having been the subject of architectural consideration.

For the 'layer-cake' building nothing can be done except to import a tropical setting for it and keep it under constant floodlighting from sun-ray lamps.

We can leave the frivolities of housing and holiday architecture in sound hands, giving complete liberty to enterprising architects—and builders—who know what the public want, can give it to them, and while probably livening things up can do no lasting harm.

Scattered about the country are scores of English architects really interested in the aesthetics of their profession and both able and willing to contribute to the charm and dignity of the English scene. One may see their efforts from time to time in isolated buildings. There is at the moment an interest in octagonal plans which assist a return to the old Byzantine motif of a building rising towards a peak. Such architects lack the discipline of an ordinance which would enable them to make any progress towards the harmonious association of new buildings. Nevertheless they will fill a gap in an old town street with skill and sensitivity.

One important aspect of architecture—particularly important to England—is nearly always forgotten. This is the provision of all new buildings with a setting. How often one sees the corner of some recent meadow disfigured by a raw new building which not only ruins the scene but does nothing to ensure its own dignity. Trees are the most characteristic feature of the English landscape and to destroy them without replacement is a crime. The planting of saplings is futile; they may not survive—perhaps through vandalism—and in any case take too long to become of use in the scene. It is now possible to procure 'instant' trees, mature trees twenty or thirty feet high, at an expense which, considering the cost of a house, is negligible. A few trees, supported by an undergrowth of shrubs, can go a long way towards endowing a raw new building with a setting hitherto only enjoyed by one on an old site.

Two hundred years ago Britain led the world in the art of landscaping —an operation conducted today with the utmost ease with the aid of earth-moving machinery. During the last century landscaping was for the most part connected with the provision of a tennis court which we, today, make no use of but have to mow. But although grassy banks may need mowing, hedges and shrubberies could possibly be improved by being associated with some little breaking up of the virgin smoothness of the building site where they occur.

We can still enjoy many such pleasantries in the recesses of the land. It is architecture in the mass which has become so detached from the land and its people. Each large building is a little ant-empire, in which men and women work surrounded by cliffs of glass or factory-made slabs, and flaunts a dead indifference to the life about it. How regrettable that the designers of such structures have abandoned the traditional role of the architect, the presentation to his fellow-countryman of inventions which would give them pleasure and pride to behold.

Oppressed by these manifestations of contempt for those of us who walk in their shadow, we may well wonder whether there is any future for architecture in England. But many of the less flamboyant members of the profession will be remembering the eight centuries of devotion and experience which have gone into our making—that architecture is one of the noblest creations of civilisation and cannot but survive in the end.

The signs are that the people of England would not be sorry to witness the rout of the foals of the nightmare and might even welcome some faded old Revival if it could deliver them from the curse of concrete and the malison of glass precipices.

The interior of a building remains the property of its owner, for him to do with what he will. But its exterior is national property—part of the atmosphere of England, a very important part of the English image. We are in the hands of the architects.

GLOSSARY

architrave: lowermost member of the Classical entablature (qv); the moulding passing round a doorway (see Figs 78 and 79)

ashlar: thin facing stones set on their edges (see Fig 9)

banker: block of stone or timber upon which the mason sets the stone for dressing

bay: longitudinal division of a building in plan or elevation

bolster: wide-bladed mason's chisel

brace: diagonal piece of timber tying two others together to prevent movement

brattice: screen made of boarding (cf 'lattice' of laths)

calm: (pronounced *came*) strip of lead securing quarries (qv) of window glass

capital: ornamental crowning member of a column or pillar

clapboard: improved type of weatherboard (qv)

cob: mixture of clay and straw used for building walls

collar: short length of timber tying rafters together near apex of roof (see Fig 18)

cornice: upper member of Classical entablature (qv); ornamental eaves to an important building

couple: pair of rafters pinned together at apex (see Fig 18)

cove: a deep hollow, often worked in plaster below eaves

cross-chamber: two-storeyed wing set across end of medieval hall

cruck: pair of heavy curved timbers pinned together at apex

dragon beam: diagonal timber employed to tie in angles of floor constructed with jetties (qv)

dressed stone: stone which has been worked with the bolster

eaves: lower part of roof resting on walling and projecting beyond this

elevation: external appearance of a building

entablature: horizontal architectural members passing above a Classical colonnade (see Fig 79)

fanlight: window above a door, often fan-shaped

fluting: grooves passing up shaft of column

frieze: middle member of Classical entablature (qv) (see Fig 79)

header: brick set at right angles to face of wall

hip: roof-slope passing round angle (see Fig 24)

jamb: side of window or door opening

jetty: portion of upper floor jutting out beyond storey below (see Fig 11)

joist: timber carrying floorboards

king-post: short post resting upon truss (qv) and helping to support roof collars (qv) (see also Fig 19)

lattice: openwork screen of laths, reproduced in leaded glazing

light: division of window

lintel: a short beam carrying the wall across an opening

mansard roof: roof with two pitches, a steep one serving as side of attic and a flatter one above this (see Fig 25); called in the US a gambrel roof

masonry: stone walling built in two skins of face-stones, the space between being filled with rough stones (see Fig 7)

moulding: running ornament formed of continuous lines of rolls and channels (see Figs 75 and 76)

mullion: vertical division in a window

muntin: vertical member in framework of panelling or door

nogging: pieces of material, brick or field-stone, used to fill panels of timber-framed building

ordinance: the system of rules by which the architectural 'style' of a building is controlled

oriel: window carried upon projecting brackets

outshot: annex to building, roofed at lower level

pantile: tile moulded in wavy section so as to overlap its neighbour

pilaster: vertical projection from wall-face, during Renaissance period fashioned to resemble a flat column

plinth: projecting base upon which a building stands

principal: strong timber construction set across building at roof level to carry purlins (qv); also known as truss (see Figs 20, 21 and 22)

principal rafter: extra strong rafter forming part of principal (see above)

purlin: longitudinal timber in roof carrying rafters (see Fig 21)

quarry: small pane of glass, usually diamond-shaped; in medieval glazing

queen-post: one of a pair of posts forming part of a 'truss' (qv) (see also Fig 21)

quoin: corner stone

rafter: sloping roof timber

rail: horizontal member in framework of panelling or door

reeding: moulding resembling reeds of a Pan-pipe

rendering: external plastering

rustication: central area of each stone left rough instead of being dressed

shingles: boards about 2ft long, used like tiles for covering roofs

sill: foundation of timber structure or feature such as doorway or window

soffit: underside of arch or lintel

solar: (should be written and pronounced *soller*) a timber upper floor; stone soller is a stone floor carried on a stone-vaulted undercroft

span: the width of a building or an opening, requiring to be spanned by a roof, an arch, or a lintel

stud: vertical member in a framed partition (Fig 12)

summer: old word for a main beam; bressummer or breastsummer, originally a chimney beam, now the main beam over a shop front

tan: gypsy hut made of willow or hazel rods set in two rows, bent over and tied together, and thatched

teazle-post: post set butt-uppermost so that thickened end may carry mortices for several beams entering it (see Fig 10)

tie-beam: main beam crossing building at eaves' level, often forms foundation for truss (qv) (see also Fig 19)

transom: horizontal division between lights of window

truss: strong timber construction set across building as part of roof, its purpose to carry purlins (qv); also known as principal (see Figs 20, 21 and 22)

verge: edge of roof above gable-end

wattling: network of woven rods of hazel and willow, used to fill window openings and as foundation for daub or cob (qv) (see also Fig 14)

weatherboard: horizontal boarding set overlapping, a more sophisticated form being the clapboarding upon which the American Colonial style is based

wind-braces: rows of timber arches set beneath purlins (qv) to stiffen roof longitudinally

INDEX

Entries in italics refer to plates